To my most
and dear friend —
may we grow very
old together!
Be kind and take
no shit — always,
Vada Bro

OUT OF
CHARACTER
AND THE DARK

OUT OF
CHARACTER
AND THE DARK

A MEMOIR BY VADA BROZ

vayda brOh(z)

Vada Broz
An independent publishing company
vadabroz.com

Names and certain identifying details have been changed to protect the privacy of
individuals mentioned in this publication.

FIRST EDITION PUBLISHED 2022 IN THE USA
ISBN 9798987117415

I was receiving loads of new information about my life everyday through flashbacks, and creativity was my main outlet of expression for them. The lackluster stories I had managed to retain over the years were reviving, turning more colorful—for example, I knew I had been in a cult; I knew the places where I had lived; I knew what schools I had attended; I knew certain things had happened, but I couldn't recall the details of people, places, or events. Ink and paint flowed and computer screen glowed as if I had been preparing to fashion this book my entire life.

My initial mission was two-fold. First, I wanted to overlay a gentle objectivity onto a harsh reality for those still trapped in the cult to which I had once belonged by morphing the cult's business model into a bookshop. And because the cult still operates across the globe today, I was next compelled to protect the public from being swindled further by its practices by describing unmistakable identifying markers of the interior design of its locations…

Now, it is my sincere wish that my story will inspire progress towards an end to the malice and violence that currently plagues our society.

WITH LOVE
Vada

CONTENTS

LIST OF ILLUSTRATIONS

OUT OF
CHARACTER
AND THE DARK

For Jack and Owen
And anyone who has held tight to their hearts
in the face of trauma or oppression

CHAPTER 1
Ugly Girl

This is a memoir of missing moments.

My heart rate dropped to zero. A bouncing bundle of buoyancy, I was born dying in Boston on August 6, 1984. I suppose we are all born dying. I was cut from my mother's womb via cesarean section. Waiting in the wormhole between life and death, a wondrous resilience walled itself within me. Maybe I should have let the darkness take me, but no; I befriended it. I learned to hide in between its spaces, safe from the truth.

Grace Broz, my mother, worked for a urologist before having conceived me. According to Grace, she was well-liked by everyone in the office and for her pregnancy the doctors arranged a special medical team for the onset of her labor. Typically, Grace either had fire coming out of her neck instead of a head, or she'd be garbed in a floral sundress radiating a manner of southern hospitality. On this day she was likely in a hospital gown putting on whatever manner that served her agenda with my father.

My mother occasionally recounted, always with an air of humor that I never understood, that my heart rate had dropped to zero when I was born.

She'd then finish the story with a sense of pride in herself for the honors of her 'special medical team': "The patients and hospital staffers asked, 'Who is this lady who gets all the best doctors?'"

So typical of Grace with her flair of self-importance and getting attention from her little public.

Grace loved to remind me that when my father, Oskar Broz, first saw me, he said boldly, "Well, it's either a boy or a really ugly girl!" Grace seemed to revel joyously when telling her well-rehearsed story.

As I was growing up, I would ask Oskar about his infamous phrase. Each time I asked, he seemed unaffected. By Oskar's quiet, passive, and surprised expression I concluded that he had by no means ever believed or thought that I was an ugly girl.

I could not recall my childhood except for certain closed bits of knowledge and two or three disjointed fragments that returned to me when I was thirty years old. In one of the memories I am on my back in a crib in an undecorated nursery, although I know I had a mobile at some point. Absent of emotion, my viewpoint alternates between witnessing myself from outside and being inside my infant body. The walls are dark, possibly wood-paneled; the crib is positioned at an angle in the center of the modestly sized room, with a closet on the far left from the doorway, also dark brown like the walls. I cried. A lot. My infant self screamed until her limbs and body shook, and her head was hot. Exhausted from a bout of screaming in the nursery, a single tear ran down the side of my head. The contrast of the tear to the heat of my head soothed me momentarily. I cried and shook until I passed out, or probably more correctly, dissociated. I left my body and floated around the room until my hands and feet got cold, or I was hungry, or something else physically uncomfortable forced my awareness back into my body. At this point, I commenced crying again, cyclically crying and dissociating in this pattern.

In another memory, my infant self lies face down on golden linoleum flooring in the kitchen of our first family home. Baby me wears only a diaper and her belly is cold against the hard linoleum. Baby me cries, again from two points of view. At first, my arms and legs hover over the golden linoleum as I scream and cry. The sensation of the cold hard linoleum on my belly is debasing. Eventually, I give up as if in slow motion, and my limbs and head fall limp against the linoleum. Next I leave my body and 'travel' upstairs to find Grace. I cannot discern what Grace is doing, but I feel it, knowing it is wrong, and I think Grace is not alone.

When I was born, Grace's brother was terminally ill, battling cancer. Uncle Colton lived long enough to attend my baptism into the Roman Catholic Church but died shortly after that. I remember visiting Uncle Colton in my infancy. My infant self lies on a blanket in an adjacent room of my uncle's barely decorated residence. It was easy for me to leave my body and float over to get a look at him. Uncle Colton was propped up, not lying flat. In the room where I rested, he came to visit me in spirit, looking like a typical representation of a thin Caucasian Jesus Christ with a great head of wavy golden brown hair, a full trimmed beard, average overall stature, and slightly relaxed shoulders. Uncle Colton didn't say much and his presence was not scary. Grace told us kids stories of Uncle Colton and his knack for music, described him such that she seemed to adore him. I'm not sure the sibling relationship Grace described was reality. Uncle Colton had not attended my parents' wedding. He was not to be found in the beautiful wooden-bound wedding album with soft, smooth, thin vellum sheets between the pages of photographs.

At about six years old, an age determined by the location of the event and my angle of perception reflecting my height, I stood with Grace on a street corner in our small suburban town.

My mother casually looked down at me and said, "Someone you know was raped."

"Who? Who?" I frantically and quietly inquired on the public street corner.

Some part of me thought she could be talking about me, but Grace simply told me she wouldn't give me any other information. I don't know how I knew what rape was at that young age; I simply know that I did because I can recall this moment vividly.

The brain changes rapidly during youth until its maturation at age twenty-five. Memories stored in infancy and toddlerhood differ from childhood memories; memories captured in adulthood are distinct too because the brain has matured to full function. Young recollections are sensory memory since brain development at this stage has yet to reach the level of verbal narrative. I am no neuroscientist, but Bessel van der Kolk has a stellar segment on traumatic memory in his book, *The Body Keeps The Score. Within it he writes:*

> Nobody wants to remember trauma. In that regard society is no different from the victims themselves. We all want to live in a world that is safe, manageable, and predictable, and victims remind us that this is not always the case. In order to understand trauma, we have to overcome our natural reluctance to confront that reality and cultivate the courage to listen to the testimonies of survivors.

CHAPTER 2

Floodgates

Therapy helped me reclaim some of those missing moments. My diagnosis is Complex Post Traumatic Stress Disorder (CPTSD), with an atypical version of dissociative amnesia; a reality I discovered at the age of thirty-five. My mother used to call it my "selective hearing" or tell me that talking to me was like talking to the wall. I think now I will call it "dissociating because you abused the fuck out of me, you heartless mom-ster." The truth is, it has been a daily battle to remember how my mother mistreated me because I have a habit of excusing her to the extreme on repeat. I sort through the trash piles that have cluttered and fouled my existence—detailing the hurt by jotting down notes in rhune-like angles of black scribble, just as it is in my affliction with dissociative disorder. I had been escaping the realities of my thoughts and memories; throughout much of my life I had been disconnecting from experiences to a degree that I lost my own identity, including a conscious awareness of the continuum of my actions and surroundings. Though I could skillfully recall what I needed moment by moment, it wasn't exactly a healthy or safe way to mentally live.

I compel myself to hold the sharp, pointy objects in my hand—and I finally come out on top of the heap; though rather bloodied, grimey, and tattered from the foraging. Undergoing this process of therapy and healing, I am gaining a clearer and farther vision from the top of the shit mound.

My entire life I thought I was just another whiny, privileged person. I could sensorially know that I enjoyed good times in good places with good people. This made me mindful that I was raised in a material world that less fortunate others could only imagine in their dreams. My earlier perception was that I had grown up with a severely depressed mother and a hardworking father, Grace and Oskar Broz, and that my brothers and I were happy when growing up. *My younger brothers, Jack and Owen, are to this day two of the best people I know.* In our childhood, we wanted for nothing; we had a lot of freedom; we enjoyed the company of four truly loving grandparents.

Because of Grace, I either distorted, suppressed or belittled my emotions, but here are the stark facts encapsulating my story. Our mother slept so much that by the time I was a teenager a rift tore us apart never to be mended. I became a drug user, as did Jack and Owen. I then quit substances cold turkey when becoming a full-time meditation instructor. Found out I was not straight at the age of twenty-eight. I left the organization where I had taught meditation for ten years and came to realize that it was actually a dangerous cult, and still is. Next, I severely abused alcohol, and alcohol abused me. After a devastating car accident, I got sober and started my own business. Despite my new sobriety and work ethic, I was still tormented by unresolved emotional issues from both my childhood and the cult, so I was enlisted in quality therapeutic treatments. I would also meet my partner Evelyn, the love of my life, within a few years' time. *Top of the heap by now, right?*

No. A new regime of the therapy was still required for my mental health as the trash pile still rankly emanated beneath my feet. In late November 2020, I began struggling interpersonally with Evelyn and experienced emotional flashbacks during which I hit myself in the face. I didn't understand what was happening to me at the time but would later understand that Evelyn had certain personality traits which resulted from her own trauma that would trigger the emotional flashbacks from deep within my subconscious. Emotional flashbacks are like typical flashbacks except that the original emotion is what is re-experienced—with or without other sensory details of the event that actually caused the emotional response back in time. My therapist Noah and I planned to eventually incorporate Eye Movement Desensitization and Reprocessing (EMDR) into our therapy. Because slapping and punching myself in the face was unacceptable, I asked Noah if we could try it out. I had hoped it would speed my system through whatever was unconsciously bothering me in order to return my life to some sort of normalcy. Once he had explained this treatment to me, I further investigated it.

EMDR is a psychotherapy treatment originally designed to alleviate the distress associated with traumatic memories (Shapiro, 1989a, 1989b). This therapy is recognized by organizations such as the American Psychiatric Association, the World Health Organization, and the Department of Defense as an effective treatment for trauma. In most case studies, people with one or more traumatic events were able to recover from Post Traumatic Stress Disorder (PTSD) through a span of three to twelve EMDR treatment sessions. More treatment sessions are necessary for processing the most traumatic events in certain people's lives. My EMDR treatment would require even more time. Noah and I completed four EMDR sessions before we realized my memory floodgates had blown open and thirty plus years of repressed recollections were pouring out. My life was not what I had told myself it was. *Congratulations to Grace and the Beescrit cult! I was more shell-shocked and battle-fatigued than many World War II and Vietnam veterans.*

CHAPTER 3

Grandma and Grandpa Smith

GRANDPA OWEN

My mother's parents both struggled with their health. My maternal grandfather, Owen Smith, was tall and thin, resisting leaning to one side, even with a couple of inches added to the sole of his shoe. Grandpa Owen rigidly shuffled around, his hair combed like a uniformed sailor in a sepia photograph, neat and shiny. He fought to keep his head from falling forward and tilting to one side. Grandpa Owen had home-inked tattoos of his infant children, one on each forearm. My late Uncle Colton's permanently-inked infant imitation later had angel wings added onto it. Grandpa Owen was a rigid and rickety man, straining to grasp his power back from Parkinson's disease. Grandpa Owen's mouth often didn't follow his train of thought. When he mumbled, I watched Grandpa Owen turn his head back and forth in frustration with grueling vigor. Sometimes his face and mouth and neck got stuck all at once in an awkward position in the middle of a word. In his youth, Grandpa Owen had tried to enter the Navy, but was denied because of his diagnosis even before symptoms were present.

Though Grandpa Owen seemed stiff as a board, boney and frail, he shined love on me for certain. "Skinny-bah-link!" Grandpa Owen called me in a quick, silly pitch, unable to contain his happiness at the sight of me. Grandpa Owen grew agitated as his Parkinson's progressed over the years, or I grew increasingly nervous for him, maybe both. We spent many days together. Regardless of his physical condition, most days his hair was slicked and styled; he wore dress pants, a belt, and a modestly collared shirt with a white undershirt. He polished his appearance to compensate for his struggle to cross a parking lot in an effort to hoist himself into a standing position. I could feel my grandfather's growing internal anger and related it to the frustration he felt when his body and mind didn't work the way he wanted them to.

I could never forget Grandpa Owen's savory pasta sauce, made with canned tomato paste and mildly sweetened to perfection. After he was unable to cook anymore, Grandma Hadley assumed the task herself, but the whole family knew that the credit for the delicious sauce belonged to Grandpa and his special recipe. To this very day, I add a bit of sugar to my pasta sauce in honor of both the sweetness in his recipe and in him as well.

Grandma Hadley was embarrassingly cheerful and though her face was well-worn by age fifty, her vibrance was not to be missed.

Grandma Hadley would call to me excitedly wherever and whenever I arrived to see her, "Vady!" I might say she even squealed it if she hadn't been so damned certain of the exclamation.

It made me embarrassed and uncomfortable back then, but I'd love to hear her screech my name now that she is gone. I can still hear her call me if I listen in my mind, and it mostly warms my heart.

Grandma Hadley worked retail when she was still able to work. I stayed with her at work sometimes during my childhood. One day while Grandma Hadley stocked shelves, I spotted a trunk with a pink, purple, and blue floral decoupage embellishing it. Climbing down from the ladder, Grandma Hadley noticed my affinity for the trunk and asked me if I wanted it. I felt guilty I hadn't hidden my desire for the trunk well enough, to the point where Grandma Hadley felt obliged to offer it to me. Even at five years old I was aware of the price tag, that $70.00 was a lot for anything, and my grandmother didn't have the money to spend. I was confused why Grandma Hadley seemed happy and willing to buy the trunk for me when I knew she couldn't afford it. I saw the joyful light in Grandma Hadley's eyes and felt her generosity. Grandma Hadley's tone was both kind and excited, and I knew for some reason she wanted me to have the trunk. It was a lesson in the beauty of giving and the meaningful exchange of material things. My grandmother's excitement for my happiness was greater than her fear of poverty.

Grandma Hadley had diabetes and false teeth. Grandpa Owen had false teeth too. I remember kissing my grandfather's sunken cheek with no teeth behind it, his face rough with a silver five o'clock shadow. Grandma Hadley would eventually lose a leg due to diabetic complications, and she was hospitalized from time to time. Over many years we visited the hospital to "say goodbye to Grandma" who would be thoroughly out of it, likely due to a generous dose of morphine, only for her to be back at it the following week driving us around and babysitting us. It was super weird, but I was always glad that Grandma Hadley could return to normalcy.

After Grandma Hadley's leg amputation, and due to Grandpa Owen's ever worsening symptoms of Parkinson's disease, my grandparents moved to an assisted living apartment building. Without exception, Grandma Hadley was ecstatic to see her grandchildren despite her physical ailments and major pain. We rang the bell of the apartment so Grandma Hadley could buzz us in, signed in at the front desk, and made our way up to the eighth floor in the elevator of the clinical industrial building with long corridors. My little brother Jack especially loved

Grandma Hadley. As the oldest, I watched my little brothers run out of the elevator and jump into my grandmother's lap in her wheelchair. Sometimes Grandma Hadley had her prosthetic leg on, sometimes not. If Grandma Hadley had not yet made her way down the hall and was waiting in the apartment instead, I was the one running as fast as I could down the corridor to be the first at her door. The apartment was not impressive, but this did not bother my grandparents. Grandpa Owen and Grandma Hadley made the best of what they had and valued above all time with their grandchildren.

Grandpa Owen passed away. I didn't cry at first, but then it hit me one night as I sat on the toilet. I suddenly cried and grieved for my Grandpa Owen. I was sixteen years old and I remember thinking at the time, *grieving is such an odd thing; its process cannot be predicted.*

Grandma Hadley lived with us after my grandfather died and before I would abandon my life as I knew it to enter the cult. Grandma Hadley said that living with us was not what she had expected. She felt lonely at our house. I was surprised Grandma Hadley thought it would be anything different. I felt sorry Grandma Hadley did not gain the connection she was hoping for by living with us, and she returned to the assisted living place.

After Grandma Hadley left our home, my mother apparently told people outside our immediate family that Grandma Hadley was demented. My mother said the dementia was why Grandma Hadley had chosen to have her leg amputated years before. The lies aside and good daughter that she was, my mother prepared meals for the demented Grandma Hadley. Every other week my mother delivered the frozen meals she had cooked herself and cleaned Grandma Hadley's apartment.

Ironically, my mother hardly managed to make our family anything resembling a meal, and that was only from time to time. My mother barely lifted a finger to clean our house except for the occasional cleaning spree, yet here she was doing food preparation and cleaning with regularity for her mother. Weird. Grandma Hadley never appeared demented. At the very least, she was not demented when her leg was amputated. Tortured, yes. She finally passed away in the hospital when I was twenty years old. Grandma Hadley was beaten up from a tough life, but her pure heart never ceased to shine her love, and she would never ever pass up a chance to dance. *I like to believe that I am holding the legacy of her strength of character.*

CHAPTER 4

Grandma and Grandpa Broz

I wish that I had known I was special and loved when I spent time at Grandma Vada and Grandpa Bruno's when I was little. For a while, I thought it was my grandmother's sole purpose to welcome kids into her home, let them play, and allow them treats from the candy cabinet. I wondered what other kids selected from the cabinet when they came over to Grandma Vada's house. I spent time coloring, bounced around on an inchworm with wheels, and spun myself and my brothers on a red Sit 'n Spin. We explored the wonders of my grandparents' unfinished basement and attic, played in the yard, and watched soap operas and *The Price Is Right*. In the evenings, we watched *Jeopardy* and *The Wheel of Fortune*.

My paternal grandfather, Grandpa Bruno, was an old grumpy police officer who snarled at almost everyone. Grandpa Bruno ate apples whole, seeds and core, as he had on the streets of Poland in his youth. Grandpa Bruno was known to get thrills paying toll booths with pennies, patiently waiting for the toll to tally all forty-five. Grandpa Bruno had a real soft spot for his grandchildren, unusual for the typically aggressive, ornery, and sober retired cop. I can't imagine it was good to be married to the man and I don't think he was a kind father. *Man! did Grandpa Bruno love me though! My presence actually brought him joy.*

Grandpa Bruno sat on the couch and held me in front of the wide living room window facing the quiet dead end street. Gently bouncing me as we sat, Grandpa Bruno sang a Polish lullaby about spilling somebody's guts out, palm up with the side of his pinky sliding across my abdomen, with a playful wide-toothed smile as he sang raspily out of his throat. My mother told me the song was about a cat peeing over a fence, but the correct translation is the gory former. When I got a bit older, Grandpa Bruno gave me bags of pennies. *Perhaps he wanted to equip me through the toll booths on the highways of my life. Little could he anticipate how much I would need them.* When I was five years old, I remember being woken in the night by my parents and told that Grandpa had died. We went in our pajamas to my grandparents' house. I held my pet blanket up to my nose, concealing my habitual finger-sucking. I played with the smooth and slippery silk edge of my blanket between my fingers, soaking its sweetly soothing scent into my brain until I lulled myself to a state of rest. I knew what was happening. I knew he wasn't coming back. With my grandfather's death, I had decided it's best to make the most of things and people, no matter what, because I could never know when the last time would be that I'd see them again. Such a wise old mind to keep such a young child's thought, like an artfully crafted trunk with decoupage flowers storing a handful of radiant pennies.

Though Grandpa Bruno would never sing me his raspy Polish lullaby again, Grandma Vada would lavish me with playtime, quiz shows, and treats until she finally departed from this world and *me*—holding the legacy of her name.

I spent the last five years of Grandma Vada's life in the cult—precious, irretrievable time. Grandma Vada was exhibiting some cognitive decline at the end of her life.

CHAPTER 5

Birdcages and Michael

GRACE LYING

MEMORY OF BROTHER MICHAEL

MEMORY OF SUNNY HOUSE WITH BIRDS

Before my brothers appeared at home I thought it strange how my mother descended the stairs when my father arrived from work. My mild-mannered and to-the-point father often hung his overcoat not a moment before Grace came down giving a quick spiel about how exhausting it was caring for a kid all day and most times looking impressively tired because Grace had in fact just woken up. I was genuinely confused but did not question it at the time. I just thought Grace was sick—she certainly seemed sick. I trusted my father. It wasn't a conscious decision, more of a gut feeling—*if he trusts her, well, then that's good enough for me.* Instinct maybe. Grace kept our first family home in decent shape and everything appeared normal, except that Grace slept for inordinate amounts of time.

My father, Oskar Broz, found stable work in his profession and devoted himself to it. Let me be frank in telling you that Oskar was clueless regarding Grace's cruel shenanigans with his children and he has done everything in his power to support me in my process of healing from it. He was stunned when I first spoke of my childhood trauma, the stories I told him stitched with his own experiences, the connections lending themselves to a pause followed by a deep-bellied-*Oh* of understanding in response. Living inside the dysfunctional tank, neither of us could see the abuse, much as a fish may be unaware that it is in water.

Even though Noah and I had ceased our EMDR treatment protocol, memories kept coming. Two distinct memories returned outside of therapy and I experienced one visceral-body flashback. In it, my real-time adult self is about to pour a cup of coffee as I stand at the kitchen counter. Oddly, my fine motor skills feel less developed. I would describe this as an omniscient experience had it not been for the actual physical experience—the way my arms and back muscles moved back then, my movements subtly unfamiliar and clumsy, yet in a familiar way. As I pour my morning coffee, I unintentionally envision a vague image of brightly colored plastic bowls and color-changing spoons of yore, acquired as prizes in cereal boxes.

The two visual-spatial memories were hard to interpret because I had such little context for them. I decided to bounce them off of Oskar. In the first memory I sensed that I had physically traveled some distance, maybe the San Diego Zoo was involved. There was a man all in black, a priest perhaps, and a large-bodied woman with him. I sensed there was either something creepy about them or there was a terminal illness present. The priest lies on the floor at certain points. The second memory also involved traveling some distance, but this time it was a beautiful house imbued in sunlight with plenty of well-trimmed bright green grass. The house is isolated on a large lawn, something having to do with birdcages, or maybe bird print on upholstery, and an elderly couple.

Oskar did not recall the sun-drenched house with birds. When I told him about the priest and the woman, Oskar immediately said, "Brother Michael," and explained the woman was Brother Michael's sister and she was in fact terminally ill with congestive heart failure. Creepiness was not Oskar's experience concerning them. Brother Michael had lived in the house next to ours with his sister before they moved out. Their house was sold to the Menuchen family around 1987 before I was three years old. The Menuchens had a daughter about my age, so we often played together. I was surprised to make any sense of these memories and I think Oskar was too, though neither of us let on too much about it.

Our neighbor, Mrs. Menuchen, was a teacher at the private preschool I attended. I loved nap time, arts and crafts, and especially the fairytalish fenced-in playground. Grace dropped me off at the preschool for the first time. I remember hanging my coat on the kid-height hooks on the wall to the left. I think I was pretty heavily dissociated. The memory is void of emotion still. Having Mrs. Menuchen right down the hall was almost the same as right next door, as if at home, or so I may have soothed myself.

In preschool, I asked kids about the 'nothingness' I was familiar with, wondering if they experienced the same and to find out what they thought about it.

I curiously described my sentiment as something like this: "Did you ever imagine you didn't exist?" I always waited intently for the answer to this first question but usually I received no response.

I continued, "Ever imagine that not only you did not exist, but no humans existed at all, and what that would be like?" Beyond that, "What if all the planets and stars did not exist, and there was only the great darkness?"

Did my new acquaintances ever think about what that would feel like? And finally, "What would it feel like if even the darkness didn't exist?"

No joke. I figured out that this was not a winning topic of conversation among my little friends, so I stopped bringing it up.

CHAPTER 6

Blind Eye

ME AND MY BROTHER JACK

It sure was lonely for me as a young child until my brother Jack showed up. I liked him. He was cute and smiled at me. He cried a lot with his wide-opened toothless mouth, and when he stopped the color of his eyes shone through the lingering tears. I cannot tell the color, a shame because they are so beautiful; green, gray, hazel, sometimes brown—a cacophony of color. Jack's head seemed very big to me in the beginning. His facial bone structure defined itself over time and it was interesting to see how his joints, limbs, and skin matched each other and morphed all at once as he grew. I found Jack's pulse and watched his blood move through a vein near his temple, nearly imperceptibly. Touching his soft earlobes was a favorite pastime of mine. He did not like it when he got older, so I stopped. I was always physical with Jack as kittens are physical with each other, pouncing on each other, biting each other, wrestling. I miss this interaction with Jack now that I can remember it, to the point of grief.

Despite a wandering eye and being legally blind, Jack's eyes were as gorgeous as ever, especially when he was a toddler. He needed corrective eye surgery. My parents had turned our attic into a master bedroom. Jack rested up there after surgery. When Jack returned from the eye surgeon, at our house was a neighbor whom I found on the spiral staircase leading up to the master bedroom in the attic. The neighbor crouched down to my level on the stairs, looked me in the eyes and told me the whites of Jack's eyes would be completely red. He further explained that the redness was normal because of the surgery and I should be careful not to scare Jack, even if it looked scary.

My parents knew Jack had eye problems and Grace took plenty of care to follow the doctor's orders. This corrective surgery was necessary for Jack at his tender age of five. The doctors waited to perform surgery to allow the eyes to strengthen as much as they could on their own. Post-surgery, Jack's stronger eye was covered with a patch—a terrible sight to my young perception. In his years with the eye patch, teachers complained that he wouldn't pay attention to the chalkboard, distracted the kids around him, and sometimes played pranks on other kids. Jack was sent to a special school because of his 'behavioral problems'. I instinctively knew Jack could not see well enough to reasonably pay attention in school as a first grader, never mind the added discomfort and confidence-shattering effects of a glorified bandaid over an eye socket with glasses.

The adults insisted Jack had a behavioral problem. I obviously had no input about it. Nobody listened to me and I didn't give anyone a proper chance to because I was already in the vulnerable state of people-pleasing. No one would have known; I just seemed likable and easy to get along with. If strangers had met me they'd probably walk away and say to themselves, "Vada's such a nice kid."

CHAPTER 7

Pictures and Pompoms

POMPOM MEMORY

I had been telling myself an incomplete story which carried me through my life and allowed me to function. Then, memories of Grace taking pictures of kids with Santa Claus and coaching my cheerleading squad suddenly made sense of my recurring nightmares. They also threw me into an initial state of shock about which I had big-time lied to myself to the point of amnesia. My nightmares consisted of begging for attention and affection from someone in close proximity to me. During these dreams I felt an intense shame that comes along with desperately searching for a sign of kindness but not feeling worthy of such a display. My mother did sleep a lot but things were actually much worse when she was awake.

Grace took polaroid photographs with Santa Claus and the Easter Bunny when our church offered the service to parishioners and visitors. Tucked away somewhere, either behind the Christmas tree or amongst the coats at the coat-check, I did not interact with Grace. I just watched. From a distance, I observed child after child getting their photographs taken by my mother. She was abundantly personable, joyfully encouraged the kids to smile, waved around stuffed animals playfully, and even coochie-coochie-cooed them. Tucked away in my hiding spot, I felt confused as I watched my mother with the other kids. I felt more than thought to myself, *It really must just be me.* Any logical conclusion, other than that I did not deserve kindness, evaded me.

I was surprised when Grace decided to coach my cheerleading squad when I was age seven. On the thirty minute drive to the church where my cheerleading team practiced, I silently and cautiously considered the potential for good times with Grace. It was refreshingly cool and dry where we practiced at the church, smelling of new carpet and fresh paint. The space was industrial but had windows across the top of the outside wall to reveal the impressively well-kept landscaping in the church parking lot. All of us girls blazoned bright red pompoms and cart-wheeled to dizziness. Despite the pleasant and energetic setting, familiar stale warmth embraced me when Grace did not pay me much mind. The other girls noticed it too—weird that Grace helped them but ignored her own daughter. Their confusion gave me the courage and curiosity to ask Grace afterwards why she paid attention to the other kids during practice but not to me.

Grace said, "We can't have the other kids thinking I am giving you preferential treatment."

Of course, I did not want preferential treatment, especially if it would make anyone feel bad for any reason. I felt pretty worthless, but I accepted Grace's justification with a *Duh, Vada.*

My childhood years are overall strangely new to me. Certainly, I've examined some of them before, but most perceptions are freshly at my disposal. The clearing of my amnesia is like watching my life unfold in an unorganized movie reel in which the frames have been misplaced. Some frames are kept together in sequences, but they are mostly a mosh of images and sensations with a trigger to evoke emotion, flashing one right after the other. I must pay attention in order to piece the information together, chronologically or otherwise, and any attempt to remain authentically engaged in my real-time life often feels impossible. Sometimes it could be fun though, even thrilling, to be a kid again, separated from the cruel reality of adulthood.

My memory seemed to have improved with age: I had undergone therapy first as a teenager and then resumed it later and more intensively as a young woman in my late twenties. During both of those treatments, I had mentioned to each of the respective therapists how minimal the memories of my life were. Neither of them expressed concern about it. Next I connected with Noah and my amnesia remained undercover for three more years until the flashbacks suddenly illuminated my intense reality for both of us. It had never really occurred to me that the many gaps in my memory were unusual, abnormal even, because by contrast I was unaware of what a normal person's memory was like. In my day to day living, no one had ever made a big deal over times when the gaps manifested themselves (if they had), so I was clueless that this was an issue, and a serious personal one. Initially in therapy, the dichotomy between the extremity of my disconnection up against the neutrality of my recollection obscured my true plight. So until the flashbacks began revealing connective parts of my past in my mid thirties the severity of my amnesia went undetected. I would report stories of my life much as a newscaster would with a phlegmatic congeniality, without feeling or color, in black and white statements. And more often than not my newscast was subconsciously followed by a comedic quip to minimize the truth and redirect the dialogue.

CHAPTER 8

Chop-chop!

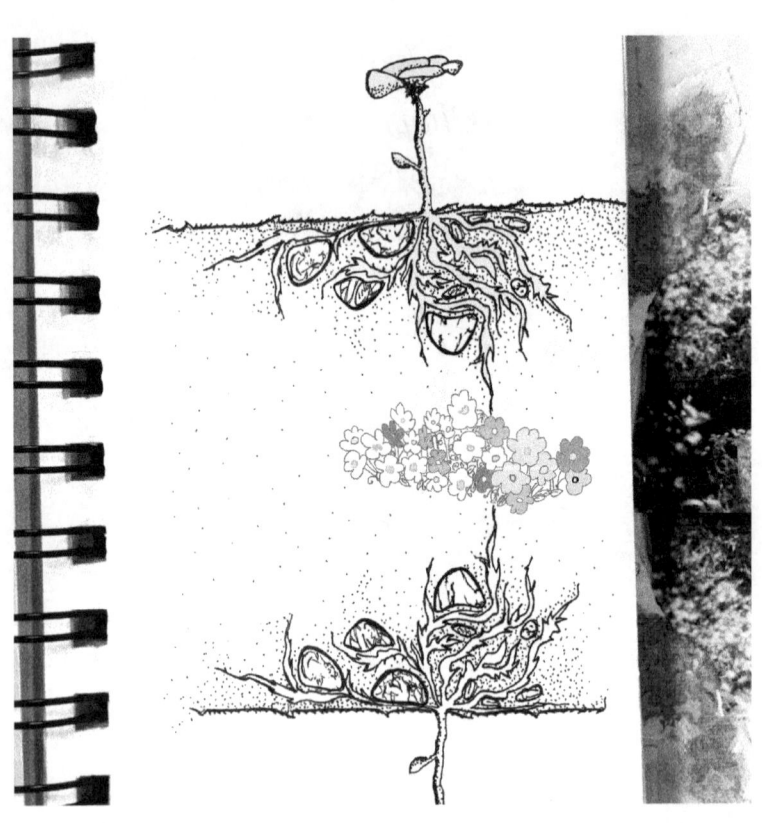

Grace blatantly insisted that children were to be seen and not heard. Ironically, however, she graciously allowed me to play a lead role in her theater while she behaved wonderfully to her audience. The contradiction between her words and actions landed me in this important but precarious role. I didn't have chores per se, but held great responsibility to make sure things didn't fall apart, including my mother's emotional state. After all, I loved her and my brothers. If a curtain were to be raised on the real stage of affairs, then what would happen? *And what was the real stage of affairs?*

She was constantly barraging me with mixed messages grounded in her good intentions for the formation of my moral well-being, I guess.

"Do not be fake, be authentic."

"Honesty is always the best policy because you will get in less trouble."

"I love you."

"I trust you."

Whatever the fuck she meant by all this!

I took it to mean: "Do not fuck up in public!"

My brothers and I always had to say, *"I love you,"* to Grace and she would say it too.

"You can do anything you want in this world," Grace told me, usually from her bed.

Now this was also confusing to me because if you could do whatever you wanted then why in the dickens was she in bed so much? I was endlessly striving for the authenticity Grace repetitively pedestaled, at any cost and while simultaneously navigating Grace's unpredictability, I assumed the roles Grace needed me to play at any given time both inside and outside our home. By nature, though, I was genuinely authentic, so I did not feel trapped. I thought I had magical powers because I was able to shape-shift emotionally, and I also concretely believed that I could talk to animals. I had done it before for sure, if not in this life then in another.

"Chop-chop!" Grace would say, and we her children knew to "hut two!" Hutting-two in advance frequently spared my brothers and me from Grace's intense criticism and frenzied rage. If we fell in line and marched in sync with Grace's emotions, coupled with rendering the unconditional respect she demanded, we were at best lucky to get the self-pitying mom whom we were expected to console. Consoling our inconsolable mother was better than the alternative—resist and make her fucking mad as fuck. My mother screamed at us for reasons unknown. Grace might be happy as fuck, but then very angry if we inappropriately reacted to one of her sudden onsets of a new attitude. If I had been a plant, the experience of Grace's 'mood swings' would be akin to being abruptly uprooted, resulting in shock. Then the plant would be left out in the sun with its roots exposed. And for full effect, the plant would next be berated for shriveling up, mocked for its weakness, and blamed for the pain that its death caused Grace. Finally the wilted brittle plant would be forced to stand up, look alive, and express its love for Grace. The plant wanted to be how Grace wanted it to be, so Grace would feel happy. I usually want to excuse Grace with extreme rationalizations. For a person to be so toxic, she must have serious pain inside her. In adulthood, I trained myself towards compassion for Grace and whatever life had thrown at her to prompt her to unravel so in front of us and at us.

Grace teased me about being traumatized and neglected. I don't know what I was doing, but oftentimes she'd say, "What are you, neglected?"

Grace also asked me why I reacted as if she were going to hit me. *Seriously? Yes, of course you'd hit me, Mother.* But I remember saying to myself at these times: *I'd better not be neglected!* and *I shouldn't jump at any cost.* Grace acted befuddled and was dismissive when I jumped in fear of her.

I remember vomiting as a child and being sick frequently. How it tasted. How it felt. How it smelled. Chunks like restaurant-style salsa, complete with flat rectangle bits, and acidic. Fluid really, until it was bile. I ate a fruit roll-up recently and made the connection. I discovered that lying on the cold bathroom floor between vomiting helped me feel better. And I would just lie there. Sometimes I'd try to head off the puking by going directly to the cold floor.

I had conjunctivitis frequently as a very young one, to the extent that I am still aware of the threat of waking with my eyes crusted shut and the feeling of coaxing my eyelids apart. My brother Jack and I had allergies, he especially. My youngest brother, Owen, no. I wonder if any of our childhood illnesses stemmed from a lack of cleaning on Grace's part, especially where Jack and I hung out.

Grace was publicly present to the fullest extent in my childhood. Christmas concerts at school, church events, coaching my cheerleading team, helping me study for school before I learned how to on my own. Besides photographing the kids with Santa, Grace even served school lunches. My mother was absolutely there, no questions asked. I sang and dressed nicely— usually in my cousin's hand-me-downs, though nobody else knew that. Whatever was required of me, I found a way to do it. I often dressed in my cousin's secondhand clothing not because my mother wouldn't buy me clothes should I have asked, but because it was what I had. I had figured out that Grace would take me to buy something if I asked, and holiday outfit shopping became something we did. Looking back, I don't know if it was worth it! It was anxiety-provoking because, although everything about Grace seemed generous and happy and loving when we were shopping and trying things on, at some point I became aware that I was an excuse for her to spend money with the added benefit that allowed her to blame me for it.

If any of us were sick and needed to be picked up from school, BAM! Grace was there. If I disturbed Grace's slumber during the day because I was feeling sick at school, then I'd damn well better be ill when I returned home, even if I were feeling better. The situation, nonetheless, fueled Grace's connections with the school staff because Grace was so fucking dedicated to her children.

The combination of the current situation and the overall state my mother was in defined her character. Grace trimmed herself fit and flawlessly, no matter what, with impeccable skill whether she wore pajamas or a fur coat. My mother finely tuned herself based on the details of her appearance: whether her hair was done or not, if she had sleep lines on her face or not. On occasion, I took heart when Grace missed accommodating her sleep lines or the huge part on the back of her head from lying down all day and not fixing it quite right when she was out and about. I thought someone might notice. Partially, I got a sick pleasure out of it, thinking with guilt, *Serves you right.* Of course, I never generated a vibrational frequency relative to the sentiment because she'd know. I can still hear her:

"Don't you know, Vada, mothers have eyes and ears everywhere, including the back of their heads? Mothers know everything. There is no need for hiding or lying. It's pointless."

I desperately vied for Grace's affection in a myriad of ways, from keeping my brothers quiet when I was younger to mopping the kitchen floor when I was older. On one occasion, I proudly surprised Grace with a freshly-mopped kitchen floor. Only thing she said was that I had done it all wrong. It was no surprise, though I always hoped to please.

Growing up we were not allowed to curse. But Grace had free speech because she was the mother and we were the kids. I tried not to curse, but it was too hard. I changed up the words in my mind. *Fuck* became *fark*. I created a brilliant combination of hell and heck, which is *helleck*. For whatever reason, this worked for my parents. My father did not like the word *fart*. Sometimes we would say *fart* in front of Oskar on purpose and he reprimanded us, serious but with a touch of silly. Oskar was often playful. He made up songs and bounced around the house on his toes with his hands squeezed into the front pockets of his seasoned blue jeans, that probably dated back to college. Happily. He went to his aging parents' house most weekends, helping keep the house and yard in good shape. I went with him most times to my grandparents' house.

I had an 8:00 p.m. bedtime which left only two to three hours for Grace to create the same mirage she'd done every evening when Oskar came home from work, except for the days Grace's migraines were too bad and she wouldn't get up at all. It was due to her head pain and the additional exhaustion of 'taking care of the kids all day'. Confused, I could not interpret if Grace was dishonest purposefully. I held within myself well into adulthood that Grace had good intentions.

CHAPTER 9

Money, Money, Money

Grace enjoyed spending our family's money and blaming it on the kids and what we needed. I never understood why we lived frugally day-to-day with an understanding that Grace was "spending all the money." We had more than one George Foreman grill, a bread maker, vacuums and cleaning products galore, and even a home rotisserie. Think Home Shopping Network. We had it all.

And "the best of the best for my children," Grace would say, buying us all sorts of athletic gear with no heed to the price.

My family moved to a new town where we lived on "the most desirable street" when I was eight years old. Grace's care for our environment at home slipped in a big way, a seemingly universal truth bolstered by everyone I have spoken to regarding my history. We kept an ark load of animals in the house too. My mother made clear that those animals were not her responsibility and she meant it. I'll admit that she'd take a pet to the vet when needed, because she loved her children and was a good person. It was also an opportunity to spend money. Don't get me wrong, I was grateful for it; I loved my pets.

It was challenging for me as a physically small kid to clean the animals' cages. Managing bleach and other chemicals, plus the ammonia smell from the animal urine proved a cumbersome and often dizzying process. My rabbit's slide-out tray lined in newspaper and cedar chips was demanding. The ten gallon tank my hamster called home presented other challenges. I did my best, but I could never keep up, regardless of my concern for the animals' health or that the house would stink. My care was not enough. I dissociate over and over thinking about this topic. When pets passed away, they sometimes stayed in one of our freezers for a long while. For too long, we stored a rabbit and a hamster in the upstairs freezer in our kitchen and a cat in the big freezer in the basement. I did not like it. I felt it was disrespectful to the animals and I desperately loved them, especially my mother's cat. I told people about the animals in the freezers, but I think the adults I told thought I was kidding or exaggerating. With the animals' needs on top of my ample extracurricular activities and schoolwork, we had no business keeping so many pets.

When I was eleven, Grace picked up a part-time job and also signed me up for a babysitting certification class. The course instructor said it was the first time anyone scored 100% on the babysitting test. I was proud of myself. Grace was proud too and boasted to everyone about my perfect score. Almost immediately, I had a booming babysitting business. I had regular jobs staying with kids after school if their parents worked, and my weekends were booked. Word quickly spread around town that Vada was THE babysitter to hire.

During the summer I stayed with a young girl during the day, making her sandwiches and walking with her to the town pool or library. One of my very first babysitting jobs at eleven years old was for a seven year old, a three year old, and a three-month old infant. I still don't understand why this family wanted an eleven year old caring for their new baby, plus the two other young boys, but I did it, even with a knee immobilizer strapped to my leg for a short while. I went on vacations with people as their babysitter too.

I fell asleep at someone's house babysitting when I was twelve. The parents were upset that I'd fallen asleep because their son was having night terrors. They definitely should have told me about the night terrors. A week later, I was diagnosed with mononucleosis which explained my extra fatigue that night. I babysat for another family as a one-off, again three children, aged between eight and two. The four-year-old, yellow-haired boy brought a knife into the garage where I stood and told me he would stab me. I would not have put it past him. I ignored the boy's threat which worked to diffuse his intention. I decided I would not babysit for the family again and hoped to God the poor kid would grow out of whatever he was going through.

When I was fourteen I worked a daytime job on Saturdays answering the phone at a local jazz-bar-restaurant taking reservations and giving driving directions, a job I'd taken over from a friend. It was boring, but the chef made me whatever I wanted to eat and I kept myself entertained watching daytime television in the bar, helping myself to bottomless beverages courtesy of the soda gun. The place was closed when I was there; I was getting paid, and it was an okay gig for a while. I did not love whatever the smell was after the floor was mopped, but surely by the time guests arrived the place would be filled with succulent nose-charming aromas of the chef's creations and the bar would overflow with a river of splashy musical notes.

I had always wanted to work at my favorite coffee shop. When I turned sixteen I applied, interviewed, and got the job. The hours were better than babysitting and I dropped the Saturday gig. The coffee shop was fast-paced; there was plenty to do, and I liked the people with whom I worked. I made friends of all ages, backgrounds, and temperaments. I learned about people at the coffee shop: people with accents from different countries, gay people and transgender people, happy people and complaining people, jokesters and crackpots, old and young. We found ways to work well together and enjoyed each other.

Because I worked, I earned and saved bunches of money. Though I still asked my parents to pay for school necessities, having my own money freed me from the guilt of spending my family's money. It seemed that Grace always found an opportunity to spend money—if it was to be spent, then Grace was on board. For proms I was sun-kissed with an up-do and makeup, complete with French-manicured acrylic finger nails and matching pedicure. Grace drove me to the shops and spas and paid for services. More precisely, Oskar paid. It was a continued pattern of her holiday outfit shopping. Grace would buy me pretty much any dress I wanted. I was more mindful of the prices than she was. And it makes sense to me now that when my father asked about the charges—and he always did—Grace told him it was my fault. That was the caveat. I got the dress and some other gross bling-bling thing to go along with it, and Grace effectively deflected blame for spending from herself onto me. I didn't feel Oskar was angry at me though. Grace was the one who spent the money and Oskar was a reasonable guy. He wouldn't take something away from me because he was upset with Grace for frivolous spending, and Grace knew that. It was strange when Grace undertook prom preparations with me because she was usually sleeping, not with me getting her nails done or being at all productive; however, she did start that part-time job when I was eleven.

In public Grace was thoughtful, overtly generous with her children, and won people over with her kindness. The thoughtfulness facade was unfathomably confusing to me since I just wanted the real deal. I desperately wanted my mother to love me. I unwittingly strengthened Grace's ploy by foolishly believing in it. I tricked myself into believing that her methodical displays of affection translated to her personal love for me. To effectively achieve this, my brain opted for dissociation and amnesia.

CHAPTER 10

Kitchen Conversation

I picked a private high school. I visited several ones in the area, including the local public school, but felt most comfortable at the small, all-girl school that required students to wear uniforms. It also had a lower price tag than other private school tuitions, which I knew would be better for the family. If selecting a high school doesn't scream privilege, I don't know what does.

High school was fun. I felt I belonged and it was easy to blend in. The school uniforms helped. And since I thought I liked boys, I felt the pressure was off in high school to appeal to the opposite sex. I did well academically and enjoyed studying art, language, biology, algebra, and all of the social studies. Everything else I found stupefyingly boring. I was not interested in most of the other maths and sciences, but sometimes a good teacher made up for the boring-as-fuck content. Before tests, I skimmed the textbook and my class notes, took it all in, spewed it all out, and promptly forgot much of the information except for what intrigued me.

I did well in school and most everything I tried. I was good at basketball. Jack gets credit for my basketball skills because he practiced with me for countless hours. Playing against eighth-graders when I was a third-grader definitely honed my basketball skills too. Basketball was something that I fiercely played to the death. My intention was to use all my energy and give my all, so that even if my team lost, I would have no regrets. Part of me thought I would play basketball in college, confident any coach would want me on her team because of my commitment to hustle and defense, my nearly mechanical ability to hit foul shots, and—on a good day—to shoot from almost anywhere on the court and make the basket. If my shooting game was not on, I doubled down the intensity of my defense to make up for it. Basketball was a game for me to challenge and overcome myself more than it was against anyone else. The saying, "Basketball is Life," was no overstatement for me throughout the seasons.

I made new friends in high school. One of my friends struggled with an eating disorder and was cutting herself. I mentioned this to Grace and later one day this friend came to our house for a social visit. Grace fawned all over her and expressed her great concern and support as all three of us stood in the kitchen. It was a rarity that Grace would be dressed, let alone standing in the kitchen having a conversation. My jaw may have been on the floor. After this friend left, I stood in the kitchen with Grace, still a bit in shock by the kindness and caring I had just witnessed.

From one side of the kitchen island near the sink, Grace on the opposite side, I asked her, "What is it I have to do to get you to pay attention to me?" I explained my confusion about why she was able to be nurturing with my friend, but not with me.

Grace crossed her arms and smiled. I ran from the kitchen to the thick metal front door, throwing myself up against it several times with all my might. Nothing happened. Grace stood just the same. I came back into the kitchen and grabbed a Cutco knife, a large one from the knife block.

As I held the blade to my left arm, my mom smiled wider, laughed aloud, and said, "Yeah, right!"

Hopeless and frustrated, I slashed my arm twice with unintended precision. Now I was bleeding. I should have gotten stitches but did not. My mother took me to the second floor bathroom at the top of the stairs to help clean up the mess. This is the exact moment I stopped trying to please Grace.

Cleaning out the fresh wound, she said, "Look what you've done! You're so stupid."

My heart rate dropped to zero. Something in my fifteen-year-old mind surrendered and I knew I could not count on Grace. I was emotionally hurt and felt unloved, but I was also pissed. I knew exactly what I would do—the opposite of what Grace explicitly wanted, starting with using drugs and drinking alcohol.

My mother had been adamant about certain things; among them, Grace did not want her children using drugs, drinking alcohol, or smoking cigarettes. I shied away from cigarettes though I did purchase a pack for a friend when I was of age. From the comfort of her bed, Grace always granted me freedom. If I asked my mother if I could go here or there, do this or that, Grace usually said yes; adding that she trusted me and when I got back home to check in with her. I always did. She would turn on her bedside lamp with dangling amber teardrops around the edge of the lampshade, squint her blue eyes adjusting from the darkness to see if mine were bloodshot, and instruct me to open my mouth as she sniffed the air to smell my breath. At the time, between ages eight through fifteen, I had no idea what Grace was checking for. I just thought it was strange and took it as caring. After the incident when I had cut myself, as a direct rebellion, I proceeded to seek out marijuana and parties where alcoholic beverages were available. I did not consume enough alcohol to be drunk until I was in college two years later, but I finally knew why Grace was checking my eyes and my breath all those years. Once I had cut myself, however, Grace stopped checking. *Good job, Grace. Monitor me for drugs and booze when I'm in fifth grade but not when I'm in eleventh!* It was all a fucking game.

I was sixteen years old when I entered the house one night after smoking pot with a friend in the driveway. I spotted Grace in the darkness of our den through its bay window not more than ten feet from the windshield of my parked car. She said she had seen me smoking dope. Grace was absolutely correct. I denied it and gave zero fucks about what Grace thought. I did not trust her anymore.

VADA REBELS

CHAPTER 11

Recluse

THE OLD MAN AND THE SEA

March 2021, four months after my memory's floodgates opened through EMDR therapy with Noah: I am cruising down the road with my partner Evelyn. A joyful memory returns: Ernest Hemingway's book, *The Old Man and the Sea*. I always recalled how hard the book was for me to read, but that was all. The novel's content suddenly deluged my mind while I was driving, and I was ecstatic! I remembered the old man and his relationship with the sea and the great marlin. It was visceral. I could practically smell the salty sea and the old man's wounds: bloody hands from when the fishing line strained his arms and cut his hands. Visceral connection, but a recollection, nonetheless, that made me joyful. I may have scared my partner, Evelyn.

I slapped my knee, laughed aloud, excitedly exclaimed, "I remember!" and described details of the classic novel as we rode along.

Next I put together the person who had lent me *The Old Man and the Sea*. It was a family friend named Jane. Grace and Jane would hang out and chat up in the kitchen, confidante to confidante. Jane was the go-to if we needed to borrow an egg, a flashlight, a cup of detergent... She'd drop by to check me out bedecked in my prom gown and peek at my prom date to see how cute he might be. There's the special company and there's the familiar friend who is a part of the furniture. They are as comfortable among the household as a cookie jar or a favorite old recliner. Jane was not special company, well, because she was too special for that. But in the car with Evelyn, I only recalled Jane stopping by to lend me *The Old Man and the Sea* when I was eight years old.

I remembered more about Jane over several weeks, eventually vaguely recalling Jane defending me against my mother acting 'not so nice' to me. I had thoughts of Grace 'breaking character' in front of Jane.

Over weeks and months, my memory tossed me around like a tsunami, pulling me in, lifting me high in the air only to smash me to the earth, leaving me drenched, weathered, exhausted, and fighting the tide's draw to suck me back in. If only I had time enough to take several breaths, maybe it would have been less scary. Memories unfurled and I experienced innumerable flashbacks. They included clearer images about our family friend Jane which secured me with a sense that I could trust her. It made me willing to risk her possible rejection. After all, if I were to approach her to tap into my lost past, Jane might think I had also lost my mind. She was crucial to me, however, as an objective and present onlooker who had spent a fair amount of time with Grace and among the family in the household; she could uniquely provide the details I wanted to recall.

Before I called Jane, I imagined a moment from the past when my younger self would visit Jane's house. I would hop, skip, and jump up the sidewalk squares to climb onto her stoop, knock on the dark wooden front door and enter the foyer through a glass-paned door between the mudroom and the living room. In the present moment, however, I actually didn't know if I would have the guts to knock on her door and ask for help, never mind if Jane would actually believe me. I also didn't know for certain if anything was wrong, so the scenario would have required us both to face a big invisible ugly. In Grace's opinion, I was Vada the vengeful and spoiled little bitch, and I tended to believe my mother. But what was Jane's perspective? I wondered if Jane had already figured out that something was not quite kosher with her friend Grace, or if she had not yet discovered Grace's deceptions.

Shortly after *The Old Man and the Sea* flashback with Evelyn, I messaged Jane on the internet and asked if she'd be willing to talk: IF YOU FEEL INCLINED TO REACH OUT TO GRACE PLEASE DON'T. IGNORE MESSAGE IF THAT IS CASE.

Jane responded that she would be glad to see me and that I could trust in her confidence: VADA OF COURSE CALL ME. NOT BUSY. DOING LAUNDRY. SAME OLD. IF NEARBY COME OVER.

I was as ready as I would ever be, so I called the number she'd left.

First, I wanted to know at what ages Jane knew me. A good span of years: from when I was five to twenty years old. She said I was around her five days a week when I was young. Next, I wanted to know what kind of child I had been.

The words immediately popped out of Jane's mouth, "Free-spirited. Vada, you were always free-spirited!"

Jane continued to describe a sudden shift in my behavior which had fallen from a free-spirited one to a markedly angry and reclusive one. It was evident to me that this shift had occurred following the incident after I had cut myself.

She had observed me then as "explosive, not normal-teenage-girl stuff when a daughter argues with her mother, but extreme in your reaction." Jane spoke of how I had locked myself in my room and yelled at anyone who came to see me, including Jane herself, "Go away!"

I do not remember Jane attempting to talk to me back then. Apparently, we spoke frequently when I was growing up. I believe this, for as soon as I heard Jane's voice on the other end of the phone, I burst into tears. I missed Jane and I hadn't had any idea just how much.

Jane explained that I'd been very angry and would take it out on Grace, not anyone else. But everyone was cut-off and I did not want to talk to anyone. Jane said she listened to my mother cry about me. Grace said she didn't know what to do because I was so out of control. Sometimes Grace called Jane amidst our screaming matches during this time of my adolescence. Jane heard me screaming back at my mother in the background. *Me, fighting for literally anything to make sense of the character of the woman who birthed me.* Jane said Grace was extremely worried and concerned about me. *Yup, sounds about right.* I asked Jane if Grace mentioned the incident when I had cut myself in front of her. This was the first Jane was hearing of it, twenty years afterwards. She later clarified too, that to her recollection, Grace never actually had shed tears.

Gotta hand it to you, Mom, nice touch. Calling your friend and letting her hear how crazy and out of control I was. How could anyone deny the obviousness of my explosive anger? It was bad, I admit it. But getting Jane on your side, the most down-to-earth, no-nonsense person you knew; well, that's absolute evil genius! People may have doubted you, but everyone, including my father, was less likely to doubt Jane. Did you do this on purpose? I will venture you did, Grace.

I felt guilty for yelling at Grace during those years, once I had realized in my late twenties that Grace must be very sick. I judged myself harshly for being mean to a person with mental illness. I had not remembered Grace calling Jane during our battles, but I do now. I remember how it felt. I did not control myself. I may have screamed loudly in my despair and desperation.

I do not know what Jane was expecting when she accepted my phone call. She revealed a deep sense of compassion for Grace and the depression her friend struggled with, as did I for most of my life, so I understood. Grace had conveniently omitted the dreadful scenario of my outcry for attention by cutting myself open, prompting the complete rebellion Jane described. The information was also never shared with my father.

I could tell Jane wanted to help me; however, I sensed her inclinations were to favor her friend Grace. Despite this, she actually was open to hearing what I had to share.

I detailed for Jane the episode of my girlfriend's visit: "Grace was so kind to my friend who was struggling with an eating disorder and cutting herself."

I then revealed the follow-up episode of cutting myself. Jane was now torn between allegiance to Grace and the genuine credibility of my words.

She encouraged me, as most anyone naturally would do, to put the past behind me and not attach too much value to the Complex Post Traumatic Stress Disorder (CPTSD) diagnosis I'd been given. I absolutely understood and appreciated Jane's sentiment and gentle direction, but I knew I had to share more stories of the trying situations that continued into my young adulthood with Grace.

Jane was a gentle, clear-sighted woman whom I trusted and with whom I felt secure. It made her a perfect source for me to discover bits of my lost past. I wanted to know more of the truth involving whether I was correct or incorrect in my information and perceptions.

I told Jane about another fight with my mother when I was about nineteen years old. In an enraged screaming match, I called Grace crazy and begged her to make sense of herself to me. Grace was brutal. So was I. Then Grace got physical with me, which wasn't uncommon. It was emotionally and mentally unmanageable when she was grabbing me by the hair and banging my head repeatedly against the beige delicately flowered wallpaper in our kitchen while calling me all sorts of profanities and blaming me for the whole charade.

Grace used to commonly say, "It doesn't count unless you leave a mark."

My mother was careful not to leave marks on us. This particular fight was regarding Grace getting a job where I worked with my friends, even though I had begged her not to do so. Jane recalled Grace having this peculiar idea, noting she thought it strange at the time. She sensed that Grace sought to compete with me by involving herself where I worked as I set out into my independence.

I asked Jane, "What do you specifically mean by 'compete'?" and just what she meant when she described my *"free-spirited"* younger self. *"*How did that quality present itself in my character?"

Jane thought for a moment, but said, "I don't quite know."

Love it. I absolutely love when people can admit they just don't know something. How fucking refreshingly honest.

I shared further accounts of Grace's physical and verbal violence with me that carried well into my adulthood. Jane admitted that my mother degraded us as children in front of her. Jane would not condone it, which I do remember, not exactly, but I remember how it felt having someone defend me and the hope that at least someone was seeing and saying something. Maybe I didn't deserve cruelty as my mother told me I did. I asked Jane what kinds of things my mother would say. Jane simply said it was really easy for Grace to call me an asshole when I was a kid. I wanted to know, through her neutral eyes, what I was like as a child. I needed her validation that I was not aggressive or mean or violent as a child. Jane eventually said she would never use any of those words to describe me as a child; but, yes, from about age sixteen to eighteen I was a recluse as well as explosive at home towards Grace. I prodded Jane further, to make sure I wasn't too violent or mean, particularly with my younger brothers Jack or Owen. Jane said nothing was out of the ordinary concerning me with them.

As Jane became increasingly enlightened and convinced concerning the details of the tension between Grace and me, she confessed that in retrospect, she should have been the one screaming at Grace, not Grace at me. But Jane is definitely not a screamer. She raised her voice with a stern tone to steer us kids in the right direction once in a blue moon, but it was never menacing. The opposite was true of her. Before parting by phone, Jane had proven to me what I needed verified: the doubt of Grace's fitness as a caregiver.

Jane wished that I would put down the phone and instead knock on her dark wooden front door and step through her mudroom. But I couldn't. I wished that Jane could have reversed the past and corrected my mother and protected me... but Time does not turn back for anyone and we cannot relive the past.

Jane and I hung up the phone as our conversation softened to quiet goodbyes:

"Sorry."

"Sorry."

JANE'S HOUSE

CHAPTER 12

Brotherly Love

BROTHERLY LOVE

you likely don't know how much i love you both

and for that, I am sorry; for all three of us

After our conversation, I began thinking I was not an evil child despite Grace's indoctrination. I was also stunned by Jane's apology. It was validating and deeply meaningful. I think Jane's confidence in my goodness paved the way for my next visceral memory of Jack. I often wrestled with my little brothers, especially Jack. I was thinking I had some serious repenting to do with Jack because, although I couldn't quite remember, I know it is not okay to beat up on others, and I could not be sure to what extent the wrestling had gone.

I suddenly turned to my lovely partner Evelyn on the couch while we were watching television. I slid one arm behind her and one arm under her thighs. I slid my arms all the way so I could interlace my fingers on the other side of her. It was strange because I was definitely having a flashback but was also enjoying myself and it felt natural. I locked my arms and body in place and leaned all my weight back gently, but fully, so I was on my back and Evelyn was hoisted and curled up on me. I remembered doing this to Jack. If it had been Jack, I would next tickle the crap out of him until he cried, "Mercy!" That was our basic rule; you call, "Mercy!" and whatever it is, it stops. I remembered Jack laughing and smiling, and it crossed my mind, *maybe Jack does know how much I love him*. It gave me hope at least. I did not tickle Evelyn because she doesn't like it at all, but she was smiling and happy in the silliness of it anyway; and I remembered the same feeling with Jack.

I was worried I had been too cruel to my brother Jack despite what Jane had observed. Most of my recovered memories with Jack overwhelmed me with happiness and love for him. I grieved over my brother—the lost love of my life—without actually having lost him, yet it was I who had forgotten him. The realization choked me like a hard bitter pill lodged in my throat. Besides wrestling, my brother Jack and I challenged each other to impossible things at home and in the neighborhood. We'd try things out and frequently succeed. To me, my brother Jack was especially amazing. I feel that more than I can prove in any details from memory. It is both a heartbreaking and heartwarming process for me to remember Jack. My mind can barely wrap itself around the amount of connection between two people—kindred spirits in the intimacy of a young sibling relationship. I am almost certain it is astounding. It feels astounding. It is hard to believe that the person rising in my memory still walks the earth; my head falls slightly down and towards the right; my mind goes quite blank and silent. Staring, I mostly feel sadness.

I wish I could tell the entire world all at once how Jack is the loveliest human being—kind, loving, smart, and thoughtful. We both struggle with what I now understand as symptoms of CPTSD. I hope one day Jack will know for himself that our shame-provoking reactions stem from the incredible adaptability of our brains to survive by whatever means necessary. Our reactions were developed for the reason that we needed them to cope with Grace's *Chop-chop!* impulses, and that it sucks that we need to deal with the repercussions now as adults.

I have found it highly embarrassing and shameful, in sharp contrast to the person I think I usually am, which is much the same as I view my brother. It is always disappointing when I get sucked into an emotional flashback and act out like a lunatic, punching myself in the face in a desperate attempt to punish myself for existing. I grapple to rein myself in and protect others from the monstrosity of my unforgivable self by trying my hardest to disappear. I push loved ones far away where they don't have to deal with me anymore. Thankfully all of this improves with the appropriate care.

CHAPTER 13

Friends and Foes

BOYFRIEND / WALTER

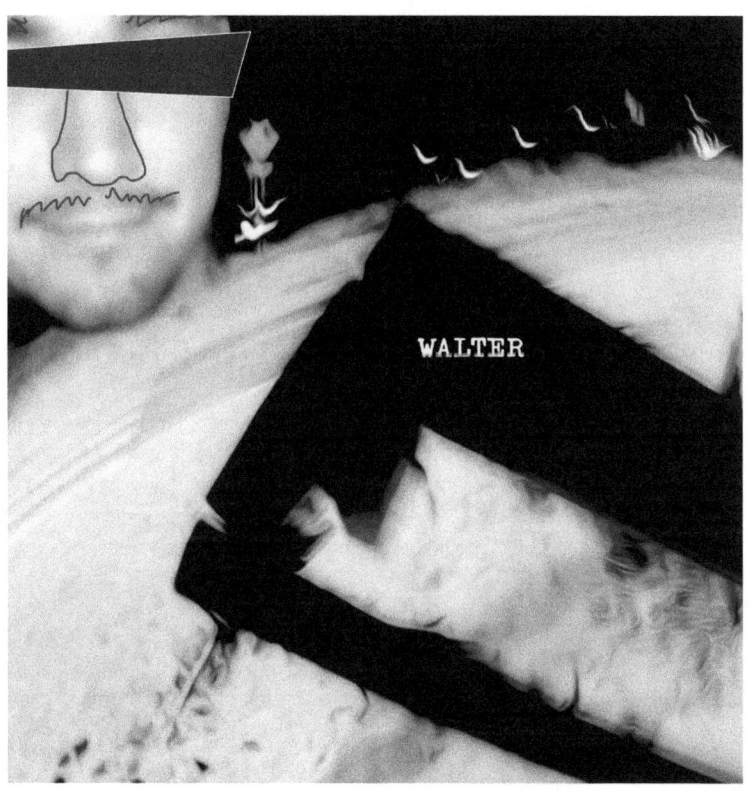

I barely made it through my first year of college. I selected a state university because it was less expensive than out-of-state schools, and I didn't mind the campus vibe. I got a 'D' for the first time ever, in Calculus. I was used to As and Bs. It was not easy to fly by the seat of my pants in college. I did wonderfully in classes that I liked and horribly in subjects boring to me or that I simply did not understand no matter how many notes I took.

I lived on campus and worked off campus. This was a mistake. It was too much. I had a car payment that Grace had co-signed. Oskar originally said yes to a four wheel drive vehicle for safety, thought about it overnight, realized it was not good for a freshman in college to shoulder a car payment, but it was already done. *Any chance to spend, truly, Grace, in a flash.* To be fair, I think Grace was trying to connect with me and be my friend and be a cool mom or whatever. In this case, I do not think it was malicious, no. Lacking logical discernment, yes.

Dorm life was fun. I had two roommates, Xena and Penelope. We were different from one another but got along well and laughed a lot. Xena was wildly fun. When Xena came in from a party at 3:00 a.m., I woke to enthusiastic dancing comparable to Carlton's dance style from *Fresh Prince.* But unlike Carlton; she was drunk, a white girl, and wearing her underwear and a t-shirt. I had a perfect view of the debacle from my loft bed. Xena liked making people happy and she succeeded with me. Penelope, on the other hand, was innocent. Xena and I encouraged Penelope as she stretched the bounds of her autonomy. When Penelope had sex for the first time, we were all quite excited for her in the dorm room. I was a bit of a hippie;

Xena was an athlete; Penelope was a sweet pure Italian girl. Actually, Penelope was quite a bit like my Evelyn.

I made new friends working at the coffee shop near school and broke up with my second real high school boyfriend. When he visited me at school it was obviously solely for sex, and I started dating this other guy named Walter. Walter, muscular dark Italian with a killer smile and a tongue ring, lived off campus; he and his friends called each other "doctor" because they all attended the university for a minimum of seven years. I met him when I was looking for marijuana. Walter turned out to be the go-to guy who knew "the people who could get you what you wanted." He also threw the best off-campus parties. I got drunk for the first time and loved how shitty I felt in the morning, especially once I started smoking cigarettes.

Walter was an alcoholic and did not try to hide it. He knew he was trouble and begged me to leave him because he thought I was good and didn't deserve to be around him. I knew Walter was trouble, but I really liked him, valued his honesty, and he seemed to value me. Walter may have been the first person I felt true tenderness from intimately. I had already lost my virginity at sixteen. I was bedridden, tonsils out, mind fuzzy on Percocet when my first high school boyfriend decided it would be good to have sex with me on his birthday. He attended one of the private all-boy schools in the area and definitely loved me in a pure Romeo and Juliet sense—we were teenage loves—complete with cologne-misted love letters delivered by mutual friends who attended my private all-girl school. And I think he just adored me for whatever reason. *I would not be surprised if Grace had nudged him. I know, this sounds awful; it might actually be awful. But maybe it has something to do with the fact that I somehow knew what rape was when I was only six years old! I had clearly remembered that occasion when Grace had mentioned to me that someone had been raped. Who talks of that with a six year old?* It was definitely not how I wanted my first experience of sex to happen. I was still sick and my breath dank from my throat healing. I turned my head for the whole thing. There was no tenderness or pleasure on my end. I think I let it happen because at some point I had wanted to have sex with this young man. By the time Walter entered the picture I was no longer *pure*, at least, that is how I thought. As crazy an alcoholic as Walter was, ready to fist fight anyone—including his own reflection—he was always sweet with me.

Walter, of the men I have been with in my life, you are the one I felt most loved by. I knew you wanted to be present with me, especially when you were sober. I hope you figured things out and made a good life for yourself. I am sorry for anything I did wrong in our relationship. I definitely made mistakes that I would take back if I could.

It was morning. Walter and I had fallen asleep on his couch the night before. We were awake but not having sex, maybe, but what stands out is how Walter touched my back with his thick rough fingers. It was lovely. I closed my eyes and felt it. It wasn't sexual; it was loving, and I liked it. Suddenly, at the apartment door, someone banged and yelled in desperation. Walter recognized the frantic voice and got up to open the door. His friend burst into the apartment, his face bloodied, yelling about people breaking into his apartment armed with uzis. They had beaten up him and his roommates, tied them up, and stolen their drugs. I didn't move from the couch, just pulled a blanket up over my chest. It was crazy scary at the time, but I'd still forgotten about it, just like most everything else.

A friend of mine named Nora worked with me at the off-campus coffee shop near school. *Nora, I wish I could use your real name here because I cannot remember your last name and I cannot find you. I know your face though, and your voice. You were funny and smiled a lot. I liked your personality and enjoyed our friendship. I found a birthday card from you tucked inside a book cover. Amazing that I still have the card because I threw away my belongings in 2004, except for the book with your card tucked in it and a floral decoupage trunk that my Grandma Hadley had given me when I was very little. Nora, you saw me at my very worst in my drug abuse. I remember being out of my mind in your silver Pontiac. I think I scared you. I was on a lot of drugs, and I am very sorry. We never spoke after that. I understood why and still do. I hope you are happy in your life and figured things out with that boyfriend of yours whom I never liked. If he dropped the tough-guy act, I could totally see teddy bear potential in him. I hope you read this.*

Finishing up my first year of college I was working, drinking, smoking, and occasionally eating psychedelic mushrooms; no cocaine to tip me over the crumbling edge of my sanity yet. Grace called to inform me she was applying for a job at the coffee shop where I worked back home, and planned to work with me and my friends when I returned from school. *Like, what the actual fuck, Mom?* I thought Grace was joking, but she was serious. She could not understand why I was okay with Jack working at the coffee shop with me but not her. I told Grace I would stay away from home if she followed through, and Grace confirmed she would absolutely, without a doubt, apply for the job. I did not know where I was going to live, but it was not going to be at Grace and Oskar Broz's house.

Ruth from work offered me a room at her place, and she wouldn't think of charging me rent. Not a cent! It was a quaint single family home in the suburbs. I think Ruth loved me. I loved her and her family too. I lived with Ruth and her two teenagers, both younger than me. Ruth's daughter, Samantha, loved me. Like a sister, I'd guess, or a dear friend, or God forbid, a role model!

I'm sorry I wasn't capable of that sort of love at the time, Sam. I had no idea what it was, the happiness and tenderness and camaraderie we had. It was real, and I can still feel it now. Remember when we splashed in the puddles in the neighborhood across the street after that rain? We had such a good time. Ruth, sorry for buying Sam cigarettes. Guilty, in case I ever denied it, which I think I did.

Ruth was divorced and had a boyfriend named Judas. What a douche canoe! I was not fooled by Judas, as manipulative and sneaky as he was, but Judas knew I was not fooled and perceived a threat in me. I knew that he knew that I knew. Ruth had no idea. I think Ruth married the big and tall, curlicue silver-haired Judas with a face flushed by alcohol and about to burst from consuming copious amounts of red meat.

Judas did not like having me around. Lucky for him, my pot-smoking and alcohol use at this point, though truly not too bad yet, gave him enough material to create a thread of doubt for Ruth regarding my character. Here is how it went down:

Ruth and Judas frequently threw parties at Ruth's house —always nicely done with food, snacks, and quality beverages for adults. Ruth knew I drank at parties with friends and when there was a party going on, Ruth seemed okay about me drinking at her place. On at least one occasion, a drunken Judas put his arm around me and walked with me a few steps in the lush grass of the well-groomed yard among tasteful outdoor string lights, people, tables, and the grill.

Judas' facial expressions conveyed a speaker of a nice conversation, but Judas' actual words conveyed a brute with a mean attitude: "Don't screw this up for me with Ruth."

I played along and smiled back. I was afraid of Judas, but fuck if I would let him know it. Transforming my fear into wit, I brushed Judas off with a joke, letting Judas know that I saw what he was doing.

On a beautifully bright and soft summer day, Judas came to Ruth's house when he knew I was the only one there. Judas knocked on the front door way too many times and I heard him talking on the phone outside. Funny thing was, as far as Ruth knew, Judas didn't *have* a cellphone—clearly bullshit considering his profession. My car was out front. I hid on the off chance that Judas would think that I was actually out and only my car was there. I limited myself to a few calculated peers through a remote window so as to avoid detection. Mostly I listened, perfectly still. I considered if it was Ruth's ex-husband outside, but it was not. I start to dissociate as I write and doubt shadows my mind, I think because I so much want to be wrong for Ruth's sake.

After Judas' surprise visit to Ruth's house, maybe that same week, I headed out to see my friend Nora in the evening. I saw Judas parked down the street on the cul-de-sac in his white Buick sedan. I knew it was Judas but left space for doubt. Judas was manipulative and creepy, but in my opinion, he was also stupid and sucked at his own game. I turned my headlights on and began driving and so did the white Buick. *Shocking! Good one Judas!* I drove a couple of blocks following the speed limit then turned into a neighborhood I knew well. At this point, I still wanted to give Judas the benefit of the doubt, but sure enough the car followed me into the next neighborhood. Laughing a little to myself, I slowed way down without stopping, and Judas kept his distance! *What a dumbass!* I threw my car into park in the middle of the street and prepared to run and confront him. Judas put it in reverse and left. There were plenty of places to turn around, including a playground with a parking lot and breaks in the median. I suppose it might *not* have been Judas but just another creep in a white Buick who happened to follow me at a distance from the dead-end neighborhood directly into the adjacent neighborhood. I can't be 100% sure. The part I am certain about is one of my last interactions with Judas.

Judas was at Ruth's house with two of the neighbors waiting for Ruth to arrive from wherever she was at the time. Judas and the neighbors were drinking in the kitchen, as per usual. It was rare if Judas was *not* drinking. I was headed out, but for the sake of the neighbors, offered a hello and goodbye. Judas said something, an attempt to snidely slide in a threat before I left without the neighbors noticing, right in front of them. I said something really smart back, joking in our way, also so the neighbors wouldn't notice we were being anything but funny with each other. But, my joke had struck the wrong chord in Judas. He could not control himself and smacked me in the face in front of the neighbors who sat at the kitchen table directly facing us. I smugly told Judas that Ruth was going to be upset. Addressing the neighbors at the kitchen table, I asked if they saw

Judas hit me. They shrugged. I went into the bathroom to see if Judas had left a mark, and there was his rosy handprint on my cheek. *Stupid fuck! Grace always said to never leave a mark.*

This perplexed me as to what I should do next. I knew Ruth loved Judas and was happy to be with him, but I was worried for her as well as her kids. If Judas smacked me so easily in front of witnesses, what would stop him from doing it, or something even worse, to Ruth or the kids? I sat on it, finally deciding it was better to tell Ruth the truth, despite possible personal recriminations and rejection. I sat on the bed in the room Ruth was letting me stay in for the summer and for however long I wanted. Ruth was kind, most always, funny too as she danced around to Joni Mitchell at home. I told Ruth I had something to tell her. She sat on the bed with me and listened. I was maybe shaking a little and maybe stuttering some. Even if I tried not to show it, I was very nervous about the conversation. I knew after I had shared the information with Ruth about Judas our relationship could definitely change.

I told Ruth about Judas visiting the house, following me, and smacking me in the face. I do not think I mentioned the verbal threats. Ruth obviously had her doubts and said she would talk to Judas. I suggested Ruth also speak with the neighbors who had witnessed Judas slapping me. A day or two later Ruth came to my room. She said she had spoken with Judas, who said I was a "mixed-up kid" and that none of what I said was true. *Of course, he fucking did! And it wasn't totally false—I absolutely was a mixed-up kid.*

Still hopeful, I asked Ruth, "What about the neighbors? What did they say?"

"They said it never happened."

Maybe they were afraid of Judas too, or maybe Ruth was too? I still cannot believe the neighbors lied. And I still cannot believe this ever happened. Judas' slap is something I have never forgotten, even in dissociative amnesia, though the memories are more visceral and detailed now that the amnesia is clearing.

Summer was all but gone. I decided to go home and enroll in a local college.

Walter phoned me out of the blue and invited me to a wedding. We were not dating anymore, but I went with Walter to the wedding in Buffalo, New York. *Ever been to Buffalo, suicide capital of the world? It is impressively depressing there.* There was a fight the night before the wedding ceremony at the hotel bar where I was somehow damn near bulldozed over, even though I saw it coming. The bar was set up like an amphitheater —bar in the center, then a level of space around it, and finally a raised level with tables and chairs. The bar was nice, spacious, decorated with gold and red. I was standing on the raised level. The fight escalated fast. It was like watching a cartoon where the fighting characters turn into an unidentifiable blur spinning around each other with feet and hands poking out from the mess now and again. The mess floated up to where I was, knocking me to the ground under a pile of people. Luckily, the pile moved along just as quickly as it had come. That was the first night I tried cocaine. In the morning, the wedding party hit the bar again. The groom was carried by two groomsmen down the aisle because he was so wasted at the ceremony. The reception was not any better. Fights broke out amongst the family at the venue and even spilled out into the street. *Why did violence seem to follow me like a dark shadow or a hovering darkness?*

I returned home and finally began settling back in at Oskar and Grace Broz's house. I was happy to be back in my hometown with my friends, even though Grace had been infiltrating my co-worker friend group all summer through her new status as an employee at the coffee shop.

CHAPTER 14

Pneumonia

I was smoking marijuana, drinking alcohol, and even smoking cigarettes in the house, mostly in my room but anywhere really. It didn't matter; no one was home most of the time. I went about my life like this since the summer before I had left for my freshman year of college. The house was dirty. It almost always was except for when Grace tore through cleaning everything all at once, moving all the furniture by herself, including the piano. Oskar complained about Grace's unwillingness to keep anything neat or clean, in addition to her unreasonable spending habits. We were all ruining Grace's life and treating her like a villain. All Grace wanted to do was love us and we made it impossible all our lives by thwarting her best efforts.

After I moved back from Ruth's, Grace started the habit of positing herself into my bedroom when my friends from the coffee shop came over. Now friends with my friends, she wanted to stop in and say hello. *Fuck you, Mom.* Grace entered, took a seat in a bentwood rocker, crossed her arms, sniffed the air; sometimes she glared at me, sometimes she made light-hearted comments to my friends. I sat comfortably on the edge of my bed, currently doubling as a couch, and glared back at her. *What the fuck was Grace doing? Now? Now, you want to be a parent, Grace? Are you fucking kidding me?* Sadly, Grace did not want to be my parent. Grace wanted to be my friend. I know this because she told me. I told Grace that I didn't want a friend, that I wanted a mother. Grace didn't care. *Is this what Jane had recognized as Grace competing with me? Spot on, Janey!*

During what my family knew would be our last vacation together, Grace and I conversed over fruity alcoholic beverages. The fucking irony! We sat at the bar.

"Mom, what do you want from me?" I asked Grace.

"I want to be your friend," she said.

"I want a parent. I have plenty of friends," was my reply.

And it was true. Grace made a dismissive expression and ignored me as if I hadn't said anything.

"Why did you marry Oskar?" I asked Grace.

"We both wanted children, so we got married," Grace said.

Hold it. Where was the part where they loved each other? It sounded more like a business arrangement.

A panic attack during our island vacation knocked me down. I mainly remember crying. All I wanted to do was go back home. I honestly thought my reaction was because I was crazy and drug-addicted. Looking back now though, I can see it was trauma. I reclined face down on the cushioned lounge, crying as if I were possessed, my body writhing on the open-air balcony of the hotel. Grace lounged in an adjacent chair, reading. The bond I always yearned for would never be available to me, not now, not ever. Grace was also evidently a flat-out shitty friend. She was clear and direct in her words and actions, leaving no room for interpretation in regard to her being my "friend" and not my mother. Oskar didn't know what was going on, why I was crying and upset. He finally took me to the airport since I was hellbent on going home. Oskar and I were mostly silent in the car. I thanked him and got on the plane. Years later, Oskar and I spoke of what had happened on the island vacation. I shared with Oskar about the conversation with Grace over the fruity beverages and he understood. I probably thanked Oskar again for sending me home since it was what I needed at the time.

Once back on the mainland, my drug use increased as I spiraled into depression. I did not look or act it out much, except by myself or with Grace. To combat this, of course, the first thing I did was throw a party.

"A round of pancakes and pot brownies for all you dirty hippies!"

I started dating a new guy, and Grace connected me with a local artist as an apprentice. Paid work. It turned out great. I learned the basics of the business and honed artistic skills in a consistent and lucrative way. I thought I could marry my new boyfriend, Clyde. I was set. I was good enough to make it in the art business and, encouraged by my mentor, began signing private work contracts at nineteen years old.

I worked two jobs, showed up for classes at the local college, and did everything required of me. Cocaine became a regular habit. Friends brought me peace and happiness in their company.

I am only beginning to remember this portion of my life.

My friends and I did wild things and odd combinations of drugs regularly. I kept my cocaine habit to myself most of the time I was doing it. I didn't want to introduce my friends to cocaine. I knew it was not good. I worked, drank, did cocaine and other drugs throughout the day and every day; often while I was driving or in a restaurant bathroom—anywhere. I was hiding the cocaine which I knew was not a good sign. My depression became more severe. I barely slept. I was drugged and drunk all day, worked, did well in school during this time, and partied the rest of the time.

This lifestyle leveled me with walking pneumonia. I was unable to breathe, let alone blow a line, and it wasn't for not trying. Grace took me to our pediatrician.

In the car en route to the appointment Grace reiterated to me for the umpteenth time in my life, "Keep your friends close and your enemies closer."

Great timing! Real appropriate, Grace! But I finally understand now that you were referring to the doctor. The doctor diagnosed me with walking pneumonia and sent me home where I wiped out on a green velvety fabric couch with thin streaks of muted orange in it.

On the couch in our den, against the wall of the main staircase, to the left of the front door, smack dab in the middle of the place, I flopped after failing one more attempt to get cocaine up my nose. Grace gave me a soft-boiled egg and then I stayed on my back perfectly still and unable to speak. No one knew I was there besides Grace. I didn't move. I didn't pee. Grace checked on me once, but I couldn't respond to her; I just stared. I tried in one motion to hurl myself off the couch to see if I could do it. Off I rolled onto the floor where I crashed for some time, still unable to get up. No one saw me there—not Oskar, not Owen. Jack was not around the house much at the time. He was struggling with my parents too.

I recovered from the pneumonia but still was not doing well at all. I reviewed old family videos for clues about my younger self concerning the intense emptiness from which I was running. There wasn't much footage. I came across a segment of video where I was in a baby pool in our backyard. Grace sat closely nearby, reading. I heard a page turn. The camera was still; pointed from what appeared to be Grace's view. It was summer, so I had either just turned one or two, still clearly a baby. I tried to get out of the pool but I was really too small. Grace didn't move a muscle as far as I could tell and her voice captured by the video camera didn't fluctuate, denoting the possibility that she did not lift her head from her reading. She encouraged the baby me, telling me, "Come on Vada, you can do it." My little self tried to get out of the pool. I felt a bit nervous for that baby on the screen. Baby Vada almost cried for a moment but quickly mustered the willingness to try by herself and tumbled out of the pool onto the grass with no apparent reaction from Grace. I didn't think the video recording revealed much insight.

I continued work, school, and partying. Everything felt intertwined and fluid until the wee hours of the morning when I was done working myself until I practically collapsed, and then the emptiness crept in me again. I did not know what to do. *Heart rate dropped to zero.* I knew that what I was doing was not any long-term solution to the mysterious angst-ridden void inside me.

CHAPTER 15

Beescrit Books

BOYFRIEND / CLYDE

An artist—I took notes, made sketches, and wrote in several notebooks. Recording my observations, thoughts, and ideas, I assembled scaffolding for my world through words and scribbles.

Newly twenty years old in August 2004, I sat on a lightly weathered wooden bench in the small park adjacent to my favorite noodle-buffet-style restaurant in one of the ritziest towns of the state, wearing a slinky white tank top and beige, wrap-around, flowing, linen pants. There was a mini gazebo behind me and a circular path in the center of the small park with modest purple wildflowers in the middle. Trees and shrubs surrounded the area, providing privacy in the park despite its location on the main drag. A glass bead perched on my collar bone, adorned a single dreadlock from under my long wavy locks. I cried out in my notebook, for something, anything, to point me in the right direction. Coincidentally, in another quaint area of downtown the very next day, I was enlightened to the wonderful world of *Beescrit Books For Wellness.*

Beescrit, it's me, the ghost of Chunje past. You may have wondered if and when I'd haunt you, especially you, all-knowing True Teacher. I will be doing a bit of that here, Itchee-Ree. Lucky you, I consider myself a fair spirit. "Health. Happiness. Peace." You slimy son of a bitch. I am a little afraid of you, True Teacher.

The downtown area harboring Beescrit Books For Wellness was splendid, though I wasn't fond of hanging out there. I was more comfortably snug in someone's house or lost in a city where no one could pick me out of a crowd—anywhere I could hide if I needed to but likely would not have to, and hiding in plain sight would be preferable.

As I stood on the wide sidewalk downtown, a sign above my head caught my attention: *Beescrit Books For Wellness.* Up the narrow stairwell of twenty-five stairs I went to the second floor bookshop. At the top of the stairs was an attorney's office to the left, the bookseller on the right, and a back exit door straight ahead. I pushed open the glass door of the bookshop and a tasteful wind chime announced my arrival. I was greeted by a smiley, shaggy-haired dude named Joey dressed in high-quality pajamas and then struck by the blinding gold luminance of the place. I walked into a bubble of sorts, pleasant enough, and it smelled good. Joey smiled at me and performed his well-rehearsed book sales pitch, pressing the daily Beescrit classes the bookshop offered. There was a deal: buy a book, get a free class. Perfect. The book pointed me in the direction of self-help and the class would teach me how to implement self-help methods.

Beescrit Books sells self-help books based in eastern wellness theories and brain science. The Beescrit classes are for learning and practicing self-help techniques promoted by Beescrit Books. Joey was happy when I bought a book and made an appointment to attend a Beescrit class there.

My boyfriend decided to join me for the class. I had fallen for Clyde while I was tripping on mushrooms, lounging on the grass in my best-bud-drug-dealer's backyard while Clyde played the guitar. Clyde had warm dark eyes with long thick eyelashes, an olive complexion, and dark hair with a showered hippie vibe. We made eye contact while Clyde played his music and sang with his friends, bright blue sky and slow-moving wispy clouds behind him. Clyde and I showed up for the class together. I cried during it and Clyde had a fit of laughter. Getting in touch with my body through controlled breathing while also meeting the challenges to overcome habits of the mind and body were overwhelming in a positive way. Paul, the Lead Instructor of the joint, taught the class. He was of average height, an Italian beefcake with dimples and shiny dark curls, and also wore fancy pajamas.

The class concluded with an energy-meditation. I closed my eyes imagining the light Paul spoke of shining through me, a column from several inches above the top of my head straight out through my perineum and into the Earth. Paul next instructed us to raise our hands, turning palms towards each other, and then moving palms slowly closer and farther apart in tandem with breathing in and out. I had no idea what I was doing; I was just going with it; I felt calmer already after the tears. Sitting in half lotus on the floor, Paul knelt down in front of me and gently turned my palms facing up. Without touching, Paul placed his hands above mine. I opened my eyes. Paul and I made eye contact; his brown eyes twinkled in the now muted light of the room.

He whispered, "Can you feel it?"

And I actually fucking did! It felt like my hands became magnets or something. Paul told me the feeling was now mine and guided my hands back to facing each other. Paul got up carefully and continued guiding the meditation. I closed my eyes, moving my hands back and forth with my breath. The force between my hands expanded and contracted, moving my arms and hands without my effort, and shifting shapes of color moved before my closed eyes. I felt energy for the first time, just like that! Significantly I thought: *Okay, there is something more to this life than you have seen and experienced so far*. The thought was enough for me to recover hope for the trajectory of my life.

Tea time! We sat in a circle on the soft, bright yellow, vinyl floor after doing some silly cheer about health and happiness at the end of the class. Joey, the shaggy-haired dude from the other day, brought us a tray of tiny clay tea cups arranged with precision, Solomon Seal tea. He flashed us a serene sparkling smile. There was a special way to drink the tea: hold the cup with two hands, savor the aroma, feel the steam rising, sip a bit into your mouth, feel the warm sensation of the tea travel into your belly.

Paul explained, *"Everything in life could be meditation, from sipping tea to mindfully taking each step as you walk, drive, talk."*

In the teatime circle each practitioner shared her experience of the class. I spoke of the force I felt in my hands, the colors I saw, and I apologized for my sobbing. Other practitioners encouraged me; they had cried too.

Paul addressed the force and the colors, warning me not to get whisked away in *energy phenomena: "It is important how one uses energy, not the ability to feel or see it."*

This seemed very non-psychic-network, despite the out-there experience. I liked the focus on action and reality. It seemed definitive and logical. There was talk of keeping a *"beginner's mind which brings a certain level of humility and openness to life. Remaining open to new ideas and perceptions was the key to maintaining the beginner's mind."*

My life was challenging. I knew no other way to change it and discipline myself as I welcomed the mountain of physical, mental, emotional, and spiritual practices Beescrit set before me via these bookshop venues. After my first class I joined a membership to attend them regularly. My boyfriend Clyde did not enlist a membership. I attended classes more than the recommended three times per week. I felt calmer and my eating habits began improving effortlessly and almost immediately. I naturally stopped using cocaine within a week or two. I loved the energy meditation that concluded most of the classes. It was relaxing.

Paul explained: *"When you are present with the feeling of energy, your mind is right there and nowhere else; the exact point of meditation is to hold the mind in the present."*

This made perfect sense to me. I felt in my body and my brain what Paul described: *"the stillness of the mind, completely present in the moment and tethered to physical sensation."*

I spent my life running from the truth, from reality. I opened myself to Beescrit Books at a particularly vulnerable time in my life and trusted it. The wellness techniques shared by the bookshop worked wonders for me in changing myself. I was changing my brain to change my life; altering basics like sleep patterns, diet, clothing style, how I spent time, how I thought, and how I used my body.

Itchee-Ree, the True Teacher, exalted in Beescrit Books, is far removed from business operations. On paper Itchee is a mere consultant to Beescrit Books For Wellness, receiving thirty percent of the income his devotees earnestly torture themselves to acquire each month; devotees whom he pays peanuts.

Karma fucking sucks, does it not, True Teacher? I could say whatever the fuck I want, use your real name(s) even, use the terminology. Disparagement occurs only when claims are false. I hope my message will get across to whoever needs it without a full-blown attack on the organization. An attack on the organization would lend itself to the Beescrit message of *"us versus them." "Them"* are people in the material world, including ex-Beescrit gee-doe-jahs, ex-lifers like me. *"Us versus them"* messaging could cause Beescrit gee-doe-jahs to curl more tightly inward towards the organization. *Great news, Itchee, your systematic manipulation tactics are an excellent metaphor for other fucked up systems in our world which also oppress some people for personal gain of others! See, you actually do spread good works, thanks to me whisking your shit into pudding! Applause!*

More than ten years after my first Beescrit class, when I finally *exited* Beescrit Books, (becoming an ex- *gee-doe-jah*) I would start feeling angry when I realized it was not necessary to leave myself to Beescrit's devices. It's heartbreaking really, though it does not actually break my heart. The fire of it melds my heart back together with a natural and easy, *"Fuck you!"* to Beescrit Books For Wellness and to Grace. Beescrit Books For Wellness had a significant lawsuit brought against it five years into my time working with them. Oskar and Grace had already divorced. I was given an outline of what to tell family members so they would not worry when they saw potentially damaging accounts of former Beescrit members on CNN or in *Rolling Stone*. We were to be explicit that Beescrit was *not a cult*. Oskar at least sounded skeptical, unsure it was a dangerous cult; however, Grace had figured it out and encouraged it, telling me she was proud of the work I did in Beescrit. I spoke with Jane more than five years after exiting Beescrit when my memories began returning, and she hadn't known I'd become a bookselling wellness instructor. Jane only knew that I'd been in a cult because that is what Grace had told her all those years.

I had been caught off guard by Jane's revelations, "When? When was this? When did Grace tell you I was in a cult?"

I think Jane realized how damaging this information could be to my psyche so she said that she was not sure. *Jane had no idea that I taught holistic wellness practices and sold books. That I was working. She only knew that I was in a cult. Thanks Grace, you fucking bitch.*

CHAPTER 16

Language Arts

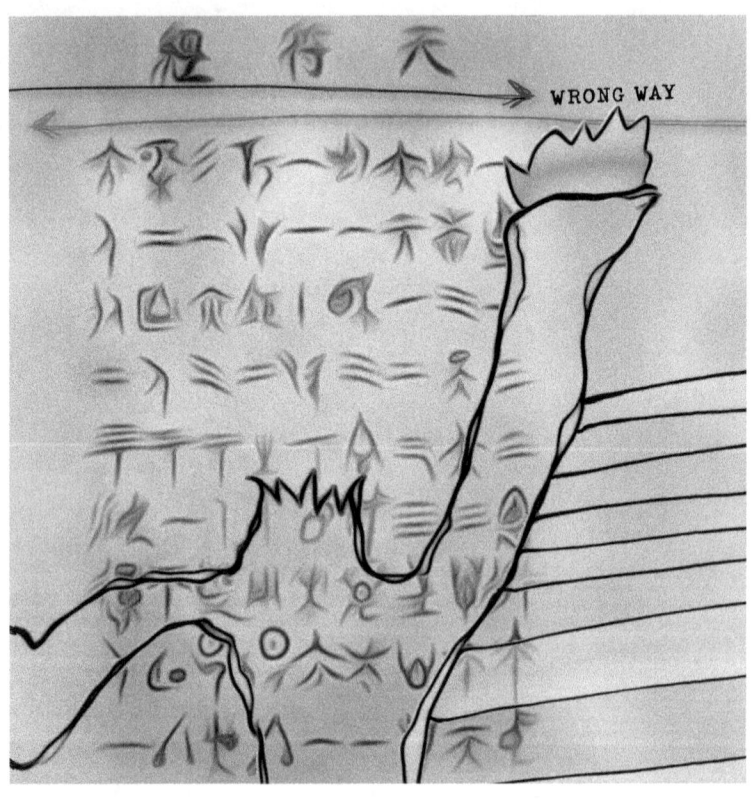

One of the first things I learned at Beescrit Books was fragments of a new language. Greetings mostly, terms for certain areas of the body, as well as titles for group members to reflect their status in the hierarchy. It was intriguing. Beescrit explained that *"altering the way you speak and the clothing you wear paved the way for change in the mind and therefore in your overall experience."* Seemed to make sense and I wanted change for sure. Using some new words, half-bowing to others instead of offering a handshake, and wearing a stiff, puffy, white karate-style outfit seemed minuscule alterations for the personal transformation I was hoping for. *Did you know all you have to do is add the sound /nēm/ after a person's name to show respect in Korean? /Nēm/ is the equivalent of Mister or Miss in English.*

I was driving to work two weeks after joining Beescrit Books when I received a phone call from a number I did not recognize. It was Paul apprising me of an upcoming meditation retreat in Sedona, Arizona especially for young people. Paul had attended the training himself.

"Changed my life," he said.

It was happening in two weeks. If I wanted to go I had to register and get a plane ticket. I told Paul I had a doctor's appointment, which was true, and politely declined. After I hung up the phone, continuing my drive, I thought, *Why the fuck not go to the desert for a couple of days and see if I can't change my life for the better?*

I rang Paul back immediately, "I changed my mind, will reschedule my appointment, and attend the retreat."

Clyde was not thrilled about me attending the retreat. He had his qualms and I knew that I was changing. I didn't want to expose myself or anyone else to negativity anymore so I had been trying to keep a smile on my face 24/7. No fights anymore, with anyone, for any reason. I understood that *"negativity was damaging for me and anyone else connected to me,"* and from a brain science perspective, *"the simple act of smiling secreted happy chemicals into the brain."*

When I returned from the retreat Clyde just said, "I knew I shouldn't have let you go there."

I was waist deep in ambrosial Beescrit sludge by the time I got back and on some sort of cleansing positivity trip. In support of the cleanse, whatever I found myself attached to, whether it be a human, pet, or object, I had to let go if I wanted to tread lightly on the path toward spiritual growth.

Beescrit soon prepared me *"for others' resistance to my spiritual growth. Interpersonal resistance is a spiritual hurdle and a common opportunity for further growth as you travel the road to spiritual awakening. Overcoming the hurdle of personal ties is not just for you but also for them, your loved ones, because your spiritual growth benefits them too. If others didn't understand, it was more pressing that you walk the path for their benefit."*

Broadly, what Beescrit Books tells is true, or the information they offer is fact-based, sometimes even grounded in science. So John Smith or Jane Doe, not previously traumatized as I was, could still fall victim to a group like this. *Ahhhh **victim**, you got me!*

Those of you in the Beescrit organization, your heart may race and your mind may soothe itself with some version of "Ah-ha! Here it is!—the part where Vada falls into victim consciousness."

I assure you that is not the case. If you Beescritters are still with me, I want to reassure you, I do not want anything from you. I am not asking you to do anything. I am not at all questioning your dedication or autonomy over your life choices. I am offering a zoomed-out perspective on Beescrit Books—a bigger picture now that I have distanced myself from it. I don't care about Beescrit Books or Itchee-Ree. I care about you, Beescrit gee-doe-jahs, lifers.

I have discovered that my experience at Beescrit Books was unacceptable and often illegal. People currently within Beescrit and my fellow ex-gee-doe-jahs will have different stories, more or less serious than my Beescrit story. There are good people working themselves to delirium at Beescrit Books who deserve an objective eye. *You know who you are and best to you, no matter what, 100%.*

CHAPTER 17

100%

Beescrit Books held a preparation training for the desert retreat for young people. The bookshop location hosting this training was substantially larger than my local Beescrit bookshop but had the same soft yellow vinyl flooring in the main training room. There were four practitioners, including me. Dressed in our whites, an air of competition among us newbies from the get-go, unspoken were our thoughts: *Who could be the most bright, the most kind, the most humble?* as we saw in our instructors. Friendly, very friendly, and well-mannered, happy, very genuinely and sincerely happy.

The session began. Paul and other lead and assistant Beescrit instructors kicked it off by playing silly brain games with us in a circle facing each other involving physical movement. The brain games were fun and we laughed plenty. Next, we sat on the floor while Beescrit instructors imparted a concept for the layout of human consciousness *"from outermost to innermost: Behavior, Thought, Emotion, Preconception, True Nature."* It was explained: *"behaviors—how you act, what you do, thoughts—these things are invisible but you can still perceive them. Emotions spur the thoughts; you have an emotion, you think a certain thing, then you have a behavior born of that. Beyond emotion, what is there? The answer is preconception, your preconceived subconscious notions and beliefs. Finally, what lies beyond your preconceptions is your True Nature. Don't you want to know who you really are, beyond the phenomena of your human body and brain, and find your truth?"*

I certainly did; my humanness was failing me. I had become an asshole drug user and drunk before I was even legal. Though I appeared genuinely bright and happy, I was hoping to muster goodness from the rubble of my dissatisfactory life and my diminished sense of self. Few people caught glimpses of sadness throughout my life. It was rare since I didn't even let myself see my sadness, a habit meshing perfectly with my new environment. So how on God's green earth is someone to slice through her habits and behaviors, thoughts, emotions, and even preconceptions to reveal her True Nature in a few hours or days? Simple. *"Use everything you've got. When faced with a wall of limitation against your body and you feel tired, keep going, do even more with your body if you can. Once you start battling your thoughts, that's when you know you are getting closer! Go harder; eventually you'll find emotions and resistance; do more. You will finally find yourself up against your preconceptions and innate beliefs. Give it all you've got to be free of them!"* Repetitive practice of this abolishment of the self spells 'dissociation' and 'emptiness' though I thought the achieved feeling was 'peace'. Gee-doe-jahs intentionally practice this over and over again in various ways, even when they are by themselves in daily tasks. Beescrit actually has a name for the dissociation they hope to create within their practitioners and openly presents it as a main goal: *"Mu-ah,"* which translates to *nothingness.*

Beescrit has methods for overcoming oneself to meet one's True Nature. *Yes, current Beescrit gee-doe-jahs, some of these methods are helpful in certain ways, but the extreme lengths to which the practices are taken within Beescrit are used for mind-control. They are abusive.* Yes, that scary term, mind-control. Beescrit Books For Wellness is skilled and methodical in its manipulation. People in Beescrit brainwash themselves and each other up and down the hierarchy, in the name of *"benefiting humanity and the Earth."* Beescrit's methods for its members rebelling against their own humanity involve these directives:

"Hold still in one position for at least thirty minutes. Tap your entire body with your hands every single place including your head and face. Softly? No, the harder the better and where it hurts the most, that area needs more tapping—again for thirty minutes, but the longer the better."

Free dancing is another method Beescrit encourages:

"Dance until all that remains is pure cosmic energy (PCE), your True Nature. Scream as loud as you can and ask a single question repetitively as loud and as long as you can. With the practice of these methods, especially when combined, miracles can happen!"

Uh, yeah, right; more like dissociation can happen.

Most remarkable to Beescrit is the way the guru Itchee manages to keep himself safe-guarded all these years. This guy has established a system for which no one is the wiser. Itchee is too far removed from the mainstream of Beescrit. His followers blindly and literally bow down to him.

At the desert retreat preparation session, we were taught the concept regarding layers of human consciousness, and by using our 100% energy we practiced cutting through the layers. Our practice at the preparation training was only a start, not even a crack in the surface, but we would be more ready to give our 100% when we got out to the desert itself.

The main instructor of the preparation session was the Regional Director named Babo. I will use the male pronouns for Babo, though I don't think Babo deserves a gender identity. Alas, English! The Beescrit bookselling wellness instructors introduced Babo with great honor and respect. Babo graced us with his presence and asked Paul to demonstrate using 100% energy, and then a female instructor, Olivia, also demonstrated using 100% energy. We baby birds admired the instructors and were further amazed by how loudly and intensely they expressed their willingness to side-step normal motions of the body without shame, boldly pushing past any semblance of what anyone would think and feel in such a state of vulnerability; even their core beliefs were obliterated in an effort to be more connected with their *True Nature*. We newbies practiced using 100% energy a few times all together and next took turns practicing it individually.

At the top of the hierarchy is the True Teacher, Itchee-Ree. Next is Itchee's right hand man, Daniel. Beescrit's current CEO is next, then Regional Directors, Lead Instructors, and Assistant Instructors. There is a group of Half-Commitment Instructors (HCI) who do not live communally and may have families. At the bottom are practitioners, my level at the time. *"Whoever they are above you in the chain, it is best to stick close to them and follow their lead for maximum spiritual growth potential."*

I lingered many times with Paul and Olivia after Beescrit classes or events at bookshops, asking them questions about life.

Babo noticed my "lack of *preconceptions*," and noted aloud that he "liked that about me."

Um, thanks?

BEESCRIT HIERARCHY

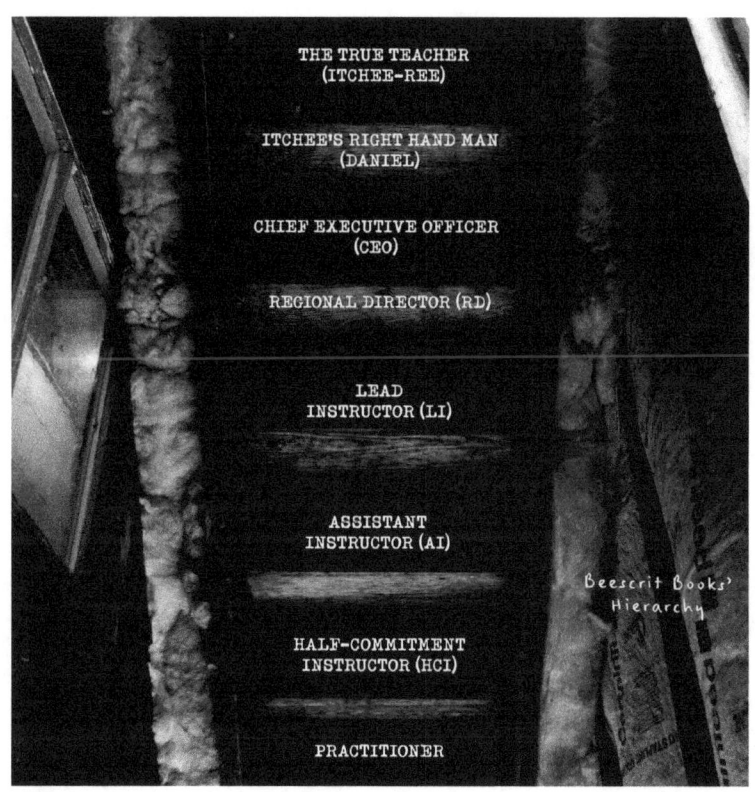

THE TRUE TEACHER
(ITCHEE-REE)

ITCHEE'S RIGHT HAND MAN
(DANIEL)

CHIEF EXECUTIVE OFFICER
(CEO)

REGIONAL DIRECTOR (RD)

LEAD
INSTRUCTOR (LI)

ASSISTANT
INSTRUCTOR (AI)

Beescrit Books'
Hierarchy

HALF-COMMITMENT
INSTRUCTOR (HCI)

PRACTITIONER

CHAPTER 18

Answers

RETREAT!

Ready for the desert retreat, Clyde dropped me off at the airport. I missed my flight. The plane had left early. Unheard of, right? Then the airline lost my luggage. Paul, however, had prepared me *"for obstacles that would undoubtedly present themselves as I attempted to redirect the inertia of my life. My life had a flow and changing course could be a bumpy excursion."* The sentiment made sense to me and was exciting, a challenge. I was unfazed at the airport and proud of myself for it. Without my luggage, I found the shuttle bus and headed to Sedona. My luggage arrived at the retreat center later the same evening.

The airport shuttle brought me to a Best Western hotel, and from there, the retreat center's private shuttle bus picked me up. We hung a left off the highway then a right down a dirt road. Paul told me about the dirt road. The road was several miles long and bumpy and uneven. The wildly jovial and polite shuttle bus driver spoke in broken English with a heavy Korean accent, exuberantly exclaiming, *"vibration training,"* as we started down the road. I practiced breathing exercises on the choppy ride. The scenery was unreal—a wall of red mountains in the distance, tufts of green desert grasses.

The sun was setting when the shuttle arrived at the retreat center. Camouflaged casitas were built into the hills of the desert. Customary to Beescrit dwellings, I removed my shoes before checking in at the welcome house where I was tantalized by a display of beaming healing crystals and stones for sale, the calming scent of fine incense, and the Energizer Bunnies of Friendliness stationed there. It was dark by the time I headed towards the training hall, a building resembling a dollop of whipped cream. I was directed up a dirt path to a crossroads.

There were enough small dim lights along the path to keep me on course. Upon the crossroads, meandering down the dirt road to my right, I suddenly sensed the thumping bass of music enter my realm of awareness. Excited by the music, I curiously picked up my pace towards the training hall. I removed my shoes and was greeted warmly with enthusiasm in the bright lobby, given a name tag, and guided into the main hall. Eighty practitioners danced with intense merriment. On stage was a handsome young man leading the choreography. Initially taken aback by the un-coolness of the dance, I remembered my promise *"to use 100% energy to find my True Nature"* and started moving my body. I had a blast doing that stupid dance.

It was beautiful in the desert. I couldn't wait to see the morning and hurried out the door, stalled by my roommate who wanted me to wait for her. I waited outside the casita and made a friend of a passerby in the new sunlight and perfectly parched desert air.

The True Teacher, Itchee-Ree, swung by unexpectedly for a lecture. It was my first encounter with him. Everybody was pumped. I didn't know who he was yet. Turned out he was the guy who inspired the books sold at Beescrit bookshops. Practitioners, retreat staff members, and Beescrit instructors in residence at the retreat center gathered in the dollop hall for the True Teacher's lecture. The bookselling wellness instructors hurried with giddy seriousness, like children at a funeral, preparing for Itchee's arrival. We practiced greeting in sync the True Teacher. Together we gave Itchee one full bow, a verbal greeting in Korean, and a boisterous round of applause and hollers. A master of energy, maybe yes. The day I met Itchee, I certainly felt something, like waves or ripples of energy colliding with my chest as the True Teacher walked towards me, enough to evoke tears from my eyes. The True Teacher shook my hand and nodded at me. He shook everyone's hand one by one as he sauntered through each neat row of us. I fell asleep during the lecture. The time difference, I thought, and maybe hearing the lecture in translation put me to sleep; but I was later informed *"it was more likely the effect of close proximity to the deep and vast energy of the True Teacher."*

Uh huh.

I cried a bunch in the desert during meditations and other physical and spiritual practices. I felt connected with others by looking a long time into their eyes and embracing them heart-to-heart with hugs. I thought I'd found in my heart the connection I was looking for. It was there inside me all along. I returned home brimming with hope and shortly after met with Paul. I shared with him my experiences at the retreat and how I had cried when I met the True Teacher. Paul asked me why I thought I had cried upon meeting him. I said I didn't know.

Paul asked, "Do you think the True Nature of the True Teacher is different from your own True Nature?"

I cried again. Paul asked me why I cried: "Because the thought of everyone connected as one is so beautiful it makes me cry."

Paul explained, *"people in my life would challenge my decisions for spiritual growth. If I decided to pursue spiritual growth, I needed to understand it would likely not be understood by others. My spiritual growth would aid those resistant people enormously by my personal growth increasing the average consciousness level of humans on Earth to a higher plane over time. One percent of the population raising above levels of 'victim consciousness' was all it took to positively shift humanity towards peace. Everybody wins."*

This "human consciousness equation" is discussed at length in Dr. David R. Hawkins' book, *Power vs. Force*; it is easy to check out Hawkins' map of consciousness there. Beescrit has used this book and theory to support their bullshit.

At Beescrit Books are some seriously good, kind-hearted, generous, loving people. They have no idea that they are being horribly mistreated and meticulously gaslit; instead, believing their work is widely beneficial with a pot of gold at the end, completely anesthetized to the cult claim. Beescrit gee-doe-jahs *"devote themselves tirelessly to the service of others in exchange for completion of the soul"*—that's the deal. *"Growth and completion of an individual soul benefits everyone and all things, rendering valuable the inevitable short suffering endured in the material world."* The concepts of these selfless acts made me feel good—like, really really good, like put-my-life-on-the-line-for-it good—raising our collective human consciousness.

How does one grow the soul to completion exactly, one might ask? *"Achieve and maintain the highest levels of consciousness, always with the benefit of others at the forefront, the ego as much removed as possible and as much of the time as possible. Accomplish this and you'll overcome the usual limitations of the physical material world, spontaneously generating human resources—and MONEY!"* The proof of *your spiritual growth* is correlated to the amount of money a worker contributes by selling Beescrit services and products, but Beescrit insists that *"it is about helping as many people as possible as fast as possible, and not about the money."* The bookkeeping numbers measure the quality of spiritual work a gee-doe-jah is doing.

Besides *"completion of the soul and healing humanity and the Earth,"* death is another big word in Beescritspeak. *"Suffering is a fact of life, leading to death without exception, which is why spiritual growth is important since the spirit does not die."* According to Beescrit *"everything is in flux. What's the point of living a life of suffering if you are just going to die? Everything changes anyway."* Better get a worthwhile cause to dedicate yourself to so as to make use of your short and miserable life!

I accepted Beescrit's answers radically and used their threads of thought to stitch the festering wound called Grace. I was Beescrit's poster child, practically screaming, "Take advantage of me!" I brainwashed myself as was laid out in front of me, the work of a true perfectionist. Beescrit Books and I were a match made in purgatory.

A palpable devil in the person of Babo noticed my naivete, desperation, and willingness. Babo, the Regional Director. It—I'm sorry—*he* is the one who led the preparation training for the desert retreat. I name this asshole Babo because he is absolutely mental. *Babo* (pronounced *bah-boh*) is a derogatory term in Korean for stupid. *You smell like shit by the way Babo, like rotten, fermented, spicy garbage; a stench, a pile of trash.*

CHAPTER 19

Clammy Disgust

HEART-OPENING WORKSHOP

Who am I? What do I want? Bannering these very questions, I attended Beescrit's highly regarded, two-day, *heart-opening workshop* held for practitioners. After the intense two-day training involving a shit ton of people mostly yelling and crying, I felt great. At the conclusion of the workshop, participants wrote goals for how to maintain their spiritual gains and were encouraged to jot down the next Beescrit programs they were interested in attending within a timeframe.

I wanted to be like them, the instructors at Beescrit Books. While writing my plans for spiritual growth concluding the workshop, I learned that instructors were once common folk, just like me; and I too could be an angel with impeccable manners, *a bright light to the world, armed with a vision for the common good of all human beings and the Earth.*

I was high on cracked-up spirituality after the workshop. I commenced part-time work at Beescrit and was laboring at achieving a list of things I wanted to change about myself, but I could not quit drinking. My brother Jack stepped out of some deep shit and was on probation. Involved in court-ordered sobriety programs, Jack talked with me about his substance abuse and rehab, ironically when I was completely drunk and spiritually cracked out. I shot down Jack's ideas and threw my best spiritual crap at him. It was awful. I was awful. Here is my main man, my best friend, my brother Jack, and I shit all over him and his efforts to make his life better.

The night of my charged disagreement with Jack, it sank into me that I was not magically becoming the person I wanted to be, no matter how many workshops I had attended. Life was not ironing out. I became terrified I was turning into Grace because of the way I had expressed myself with Jack.

There have been lots of times in my life when I could not forgive myself. In my fight with Jack, I felt truly vile and mean with clammy disgust smothered all over me. The good news was that I believed I had already found a solution for the monster inside me: My spiritual practice was underway at Beescrit Books and I was only twenty years old. *Young, right? Promising, right?*

The morning after I had drunkenly castigated Jack, I showed up at the bookshop hungover. I was done. *I took reprieve in sacrificing my life for the potential benefit of others.* Even if Beescrit's promises weren't true, I might as well press myself to be as virtuous as I could. I would certainly do less harm.

I liked what Beescrit offered me. Beescrit instructors were kind and warm and happy. Beescrit's physical and spiritual practices helped my body feel better. My irritable bowels ceased to be a problem and I stopped using drugs. Instructors encouraged me to do at least one nice thing per day for my family that my family members wouldn't know about, and this helped me conquer habits on my list that I wanted to change: fighting with others, drugs, sex, and alcohol were things that must go. I was devoted to my glorious undertaking with a fresh start.

CHAPTER 20

Pure Cosmic Energy

Beescrit held weekly, secretive, late-night training sessions. Instructors scurried hurriedly from the bookshop after the last class to attend them. Only a part-timer, I was left behind, desperately curious about night training and why Joey, the front desk guy, sometimes got to go. Joey taught classes for groups of practitioners but did not have the official silk tunic or title that Paul and the other instructors had.

I finally got invited to a night training and then over for dinner at the Beescrit instructors' house. Turns out, they lived together! How much fun is that!? A bunch of delightful people all under one roof, *"striving for spiritual completion and love for the Earth."* How lovely!

After a brief tour of the place, I wouldn't have called it homey exactly, but it was fine. Paul and another instructor named Clayton shared a space next to the kitchen, a room using bamboo blinds as a makeshift wall. There were eight people living in the house.

In awe of the instructors' disciplined lifestyle, I was wide-eyed, hungry for connection, direction, and goodness made from what was left of me. There was a proper way to do everything, nice and clear with no room for mistakes. I liked this. I could do this, be better than the previous version of myself. Like a robot, the mantra was hard-wired into my head: *"Everything was an opportunity to practice sincerity and focus on Pure Cosmic Energy (PCE). Pure Cosmic Energy is a short-cut to the energy of True Nature. Oneness with PCE over time nurtures the soul's growth, so the planet can be healed through human spiritual awakening."*

We sincerely summoned PCE while washing the rice three times. We sat on the floor to eat on short tables as some cultures do. Everyone except Babo, who was above the level of practice, prepared dinner. We set the table, cooked the food and then served it, ate communally, and cleaned up afterwards—*all spiritual practice and opportunity for positive change.* Then Babo blamed Paul for maggots smoldering in the trash can outside—I admit it now, a bit of an anti-climax, that one. Still, in the moment I was giddy: *"Everything was practice towards spiritual completion and the ability to positively affect humanity and the planet. Sincerity was key."*

Instructors are prisoners in Beescrit. Enslaved. No exaggeration. It is no fault of their own. In my case, I became someone I didn't like. I saw no way out from my problems, so when Beescrit was happy to have me, challenged me, praised me, and further explained: *"If you devote yourself to spiritual growth it would help your family,"* I gobbled it up. I would help my family through energy and spirit even if I never spoke with them! *A sad state of affairs, but better than no actionable solution.*

I am now more than five years out from under the thumb of Beescrit Books. It took me time to toy with the word 'cult.' I still use it loosely. It seems so bad and dire; doesn't it? In my experience, I did good work helping people through Beescrit. I also spread partially correct information with all my heart and energy for someone else's gain. Barely slept, sometimes barely ate, either as a discipline for spirituality or because there was no money for it. Beescrit gee-doe-jahs are extra spiritual when in dire straits. I threw away my material belongings, especially items holding sentimental value. I abandoned my career and schooling, and I broke up with Clyde.

Clyde, you were a good guy, sorry I was such a mean bitch to you. You didn't deserve it.

After we broke up, Clyde sent me a text message:

VADA, WHY ARE YOU IN MY DREAMS?

Probably because I needed help and some part of you was aware of that, Clyde. Thank you for trying.

Beescrit prepared me for friends, family, and other outsiders who would reject my choice *"to live minimally and devote myself entirely to spiritual growth for our human family and the planet."* I was fortified against *such resistance*, but my loved ones didn't fight me much. I was a stubborn recluse in rebellion, but I also finally stopped drinking and using drugs—a relief to anyone who gave a damn. Overall I was doing better, but I just wasn't myself anymore. *I was PCE!*

I remember Jack crying out to me, "What did you do with my sister?! You are not my sister!"

And he couldn't have been more right.

CHAPTER 21

Folklore

Would I choose the red pill or the blue pill? Would I live in the world society wanted me to live in or would I live in Beescrit's world? *"The material world would fail because of an imbalance of power and convoluted capitalism."* I gathered this from among Beescrit's suggested media, the film *Zeitgeist*. Beescrit's solution: *raise human consciousness*. Beescrit Books' emphasis on a shift of our American economic and social dynamic through spiritual cause is not reasonable, though I believed it at the time. After attending a handful of clandestine late-night training sessions, I resolved to become an instructor. These sessions were sacred and spiritual, physically intensive, sometimes fun, and sometimes serious.

The tumultuous disagreement with my brother Jack had pushed me over the edge where I couldn't tolerate myself, but this was a while in coming. I was bored of life and reckless to boot. I originally thought I would marry Clyde, have a few kids, work by creating art, and be comfortable enough; however, I desperately wanted to do something good with my life. I knew the direction my life was heading was not where I wanted to go. Brushing aside my dreams with Clyde, I thankfully stuck with Beescrit. Now, I could torture myself in secret behind a mask of PCE until my final enlightenment and death.

Beescrit was powerful, peaceful, and polite with a touch of sunshine.

In summary, Beescrit said, *"If you become one with pure cosmic energy and complete your soul, your suffering will permanently end and it will even assist your entire bloodline spanning all time."*

Fan-fucking-tastic, right? Sign me up. I hated myself.

I protected Beescrit and my decision to live a life dedicated to spiritual growth with the brightness of PCE. I was not myself, but I wasn't actively killing myself with drugs and alcohol anymore. I pulled back from Oskar, Jack, and Owen; Grace too, but our relationship was a fallacy anyway. I pulled back from everyone and ran into the arms of Beescrit. It was right about this time when Oskar divorced Grace.

Grace unexpectedly joined Beescrit Books when I started working there full-time. Still talks about it, proudly stating to anyone who will listen that she was the only one who supported me in my choice to join Beescrit.

I should take a moment to applaud Grace, don't you think? Come on, everyone, clap your hands slowly—once, twice, three times. That'll do. It's been more than fifteen years, Grace. We've barely spoken, and you have no idea who I am. Congratulations on supporting me in bleeding myself dry in a shitty situation and reminding people in your life how much you were there for me and supported me when no one else did. And how sad you are that your own daughter won't have a relationship with you even after your grand gesture! This pisses me off so royally knowing what I know now, Grace. You are an impressively cruel manipulator and abuser. You knew Beescrit was a cult.

Grace took a couple of workshops, even one out in the desert. I had high hopes for our relationship, but it was the same. I spoke with Grace intermittently over the years, encouraging her to let bygones be bygones between us. Grace could never hear it and instead usually yelled at me, blamed me, or cried out of self-pity. I was still the kid and she was still the mother which meant that **she** was always right.

"*She*, a word you should never use to describe your mother," according to Grace.

I left the job doing art, canceled contracts I had signed for private art-work, and worked with Beescrit Books full-time instead. Before I completed the main instructor training where I got my official Beescrit gee-doe-jah tunic—*Woot! Woot!*—the instructors moved to a new house and invited me to live with them. There were late night business meetings during the week —I was permitted to attend some—in addition to night training after working at the bookshop all day.

On occasion, I worked with a very nice woman named Daisy. Daisy was five feet tall, forty years old, cute as a freaking button. She flashed a lovely pristine-white smile—though her teeth were not straightened—and spoke with a Korean accent, as most instructors did, even the ones born in the US who were not Korean. Daisy tried to help me fit in when she saw me frustrated with myself and unable to be as sincere and single-minded as the others.

We met at the new house for a night meeting. On the hardwood floor in one of the bedrooms upstairs, we made a semicircle facing Babo who stood with his back to a bare beige wall. Babo called me to the front where he stood and then stepped off to the side. Babo asked me a question that I do not remember. I looked at Daisy, hoping she could help me, but we were both silent.

Babo called out to Clayton, motioning him to stand up front next to me, "What do you do if a window in the house is broken, Clayton?"

Clayton's eyes bounced back and forth, searching for an answer which was not the one Babo wanted, finally saying, "I would fix the window."

Babo stated, "No, the window would have to be fully replaced."

Despite this implication, I was somehow given another chance.

Afterwards Daisy found me and asked, "Why didn't you say what I told you earlier?"

I said that I didn't know. And I still don't know what Daisy was referring to, but at least I felt supported.

Weeks passed. There was another notable night meeting at the house, this time in the bedroom I shared with two other women. The three of us each had a twin mattress and bed frames, and all eight of us fit in a circle in the center of the room with plenty of space for the meeting. Because I was not technically a Beescrit instructor yet, I would be the person with whom the others practiced their book sales and Beescrit class membership consultations. I sat cross-legged in the middle of the circle on the hardwood floor. Doing my best to be of most use, I put myself in the shoes of potential practitioners so I could give authentic responses. Each instructor took her turn giving me a consultation for one workshop or membership or another. One person did a particularly good job; some struggled because English was not their first language. The last one to role-play with me was Olivia. Up to this point, I thought this was consultation practice for business purposes. I met Olivia the same as I had the others; however, when I wouldn't say yes to her pitch right away, Olivia slapped my face, then punched my chest, and smacked my head.

I'm not sure how many times, several. The first impact simply surprised me; I trusted Olivia.

Then when Olivia hit me again and I had a minimal response, I said aloud, "It's almost like I want this, right?"

Olivia continued with a few more blows. I looked Olivia in the eyes and saw the tears she was holding behind them. I instinctively knew Babo was behind this because Olivia would not do this of her own accord.

When I saw both sadness behind and fear in Olivia's eyes, I whispered to her, "It's okay."

Olivia was my roommate at the time. (We were often shuffled around to different rooms.) In other regions of Beescrit, instructors switched around not just their rooms, but also houses and even states or countries. The house setting of this episode is the first Beescrit rental I lived in with Babo, Olivia, Paul, Clayton, Daisy and others residing with me.

The 'meeting', or whatever the fuck it was, ended. I sat on my bed.

I looked at Olivia across the room and said, "It's okay, you know, I know you didn't want to do that."

Olivia came and sat on my bed and said, "I was afraid I would never be able to look at you again."

Things were never the same between us, and we had been close. As Olivia withdrew, I obsessively pressed her for closeness. She started sleeping at the bookshop, instead of coming home. I thought it was my fault because I was so annoying and clingy, but I'm not sure. I changed rooms. Olivia and I worked together for a period of time afterwards at a brand new Beescrit Books location in a town foreign to both of us. Olivia eventually *exited* Beescrit five or six years before I did.

I spoke with Olivia several months after I too *exited* Beescrit myself. "You are good Olivia, and don't you fucking forget it."

Babo took me for walks inside and outside, mostly in the spiritual training room at the bookshop nearest our house. During the walks Babo stopped and kissed me, each time asking if I had lost myself in the kiss or remained focused on the energy center in my abdomen. I thought it was another weird method of practice.

Paul had already filled me in that spiritual growth was not easy, and *"oftentimes ideas presented by Beescrit seem contrary to one another, but if you stick with it, all will make sense." What bullshit! A statement just vague enough that when applied to a given situation it could gloss over the murky and justify the absurd. Drink some more Kool-Aid, Vada. What's this? Kool-Aid? Thank you, I'll have two.*

Beescrit Books has its own version of folklore to transmit ideas. One story goes like this:

Jeremiah, looking for spiritual teachings, arrives at the door of a spiritual teacher and asks the teacher to please teach him. The teacher denies Jeremiah the teachings, orders him away, and closes the door on Jeremiah. The devout Jeremiah stays outside the teacher's house and waits. Days later, the spiritual teacher opens the door to find Jeremiah still waiting there.

The teacher asks Jeremiah, "Who is the fellow that made you stay here all this time?"

Jeremiah cuts off his arm, hands it to the teacher, and says, "This is the fellow who made me stand here."

The moral of the story is, *"If you want spiritual growth and teachings you have to be willing to do anything, even sacrifice your body or ingest your own shit, because in the face of spiritual growth the body means nothing. What is the use of a body without spiritual growth? It is basically an elaborate arrangement of water and a variety of elements from the periodic table. We could rope in physics or quantum physics; the body is mostly made of nothing, empty space."*

There was another memorable nighttime business meeting. In Babo's bedroom I sat on the floor with everyone else. We customarily chanted a prayer, and wore regular clothing, no tunics or fancy-pajama teaching garb.

Babo instructed me: "Vada, stand up and take off all your clothes." Point blank.

I laughed aloud, and said confidently with good humor, "You're kidding, right?"

Babo looked at me seriously. Babo was a serious man, more than twice my age. I was unwilling. He got angry, told me I had no trust, and there was no use for me at Beescrit.

Babo then pointed to one of the other girls and said, "She would have sex with me right here in front of everyone if I told her to."

I looked at the girl who was clearly embarrassed by this. In a rigid huff Babo ended the meeting, told me to pack my things, and leave. I was upset because I already had nothing. I had cut everyone out of my life, abandoned my career, and left school *"in the name of spiritual growth for myself, my family, humanity, and the Earth."*

I started packing my few belongings but was called down to the living room where Babo was with Olivia. Babo said

Olivia had had a dream about me and because of the dream I was allowed to stay. It was late in the evening, around 10:00 p.m. Babo was no longer pushing me to move out, but in order to stay I had to do sincerity training overnight, asking one question repeatedly: *"True Teacher, do you know me?"*

My sincerity training commenced—one repetitive motion engaging the entire body three thousand times. At a regular pace it takes eight hours to complete three thousand sincerity prostrations. The practice is commonly done in a group so people can support each other and take turns counting. Lots of times we used a sacred text, keeping count using the characters of the prayer. The point of the exercise was humility, repentance, and purification; in my case, gratitude was also a focus of the practice. Grace always told me how ungrateful I was, so I was, well, grateful for a way to make myself more grateful. I finished the three thousand sincerity bowing exercises in six hours.

Early morning now, everyone slept except Babo who waited for me upstairs. I peered up the spiral stairway and saw him looking over the edge of the railing. Babo motioned me upstairs. We went into his room.

Babo asked me what answer I had to the question I had just repeatedly asked while performing the sincerity practice: *"True Teacher, do you know me?"*

I told Babo my answer, "The True Teacher knows me, but I do not know the True Teacher."

Babo nodded, satisfied, and told me to never forget it. He then instructed me to close my eyes and remove all of my clothing. He said he would close his eyes too. I stood with my eyes closed in Babo's room, naked. Babo next ordered me to put my clothes back on and I did. As I lifted my eyes I saw Babo cross-legged on the floor at the short table in his room exactly the same as before I had taken my clothes off.

Babo was looking down at first but gazed up at me. "I didn't see you." Afterwards, he made a comment about marks on my abdomen.

I had made the marks on my abdomen myself after returning from a twenty-one day physical and spiritual training high up in the mountains of the desert where the trees were tall and remarkably straight. During every training I attended I hoped to attain enlightenment and stop being a disturbance to everyone around me. I could never be perfect and was certainly far from good enough. One day my self-hatred became too much. Disappointed after twenty-one super-devoted days of practice, I still found myself insufferable, stupid, arrogant, and ungrateful. I attempted stabbing myself in the stomach multiple times, but the knife was very dull, and I knew it at the attempt. It wasn't a suicide attempt, just a punishment for being so all-around lacking as a human being. In retrospect, I did it out of desperation and in hopes the act would shock my system into a *Holy-shit! Straighten-up-and-fly-right!* type of thing. I just wasn't good enough: I couldn't even cook ramen noodles properly.

I was working under Olivia when I had made the marks on my abdomen. I loved Olivia. I thought Olivia was the best thing since sliced bread and I wanted to be just like her. Olivia was beautiful, polite, humble, and kind. Yes, Olivia had performed those violent acts against me, but I knew Babo was behind them; and it was supposed to be spiritual training. At this time, before I received my tunic and became an official Beescrit gee-doe-jah, I was paid a reasonable amount and bought Olivia fancy sushi for lunch almost every day. Olivia commented that she was thankful for the sushi but was starting to feel malnourished and would like it if I varied our diet. I tried making ramen noodles. It's not like I'd never made ramen noodles before. I suppose that I just cooked the ramen too long the first time that I made them for Olivia.

Olivia told me, "Nobody likes soggy noodles."

I chuckled, apologized, and thought to myself, *I don't think I mind soggy noodles*, and understood that Olivia must prefer them al dente. Next time I broached the ramen I forked a noodle from the boiling water and flung it on the wall to see if it was ready.

I know, I know.

Before I was considered fully *in* Beescrit, I had been living and working with them full-time for approximately one year. In that time, Babo had kicked me out, let me back in, guided me to repent through hours-long sincerity training overnight, had me take my clothes off in front of him, and regularly summoned me to his room after that. Babo asked me to lie on top of him in his bed. He was clearly excited by this. Babo told me that *"if I truly wanted to open my heart and grow spiritually,"* I could have a sexual relationship with him.

I thought about it, especially since Paul was pursuing me at the same time. Paul was close with Babo and respected him. Paul told me that Babo was encouraging him to explore a relationship with me. Both Babo and Paul were looking for a physical relationship with me at the same time for different reasons, and Babo was aware of Paul's intentions, but Paul didn't know Babo's. Before I made my 'decision' to engage sexually with Babo, I asked Olivia if it was part of spiritual practice in

Beescrit to not attach to one person, but to have several sexual relationships at once. Olivia was taken aback by my question, and said something in line with Beescrit messaging.

My understanding was that *"spiritual growth was difficult and necessitated pushing the limits of your mind and body, using every single thing you've got towards Beescrit's goal of benefiting your family, humanity, the Earth, and consequently yourself."* Engaging in sex seemed a small price for *spiritual growth and enlightenment,* so I 'agreed' to have sexual interactions with Babo. *My heart rate should have dropped to zero! I'd be surprised if I had even a faint pulse during this time.* I am happy that in a mutually compliant relationship, Paul and I never had sex. It was better for both of us.

Paul *exited* Beescrit Books For Wellness.

Before doing so, he had told me, "Do not leave Beescrit no matter what, even if I do."

He called me a decade later to apologize.

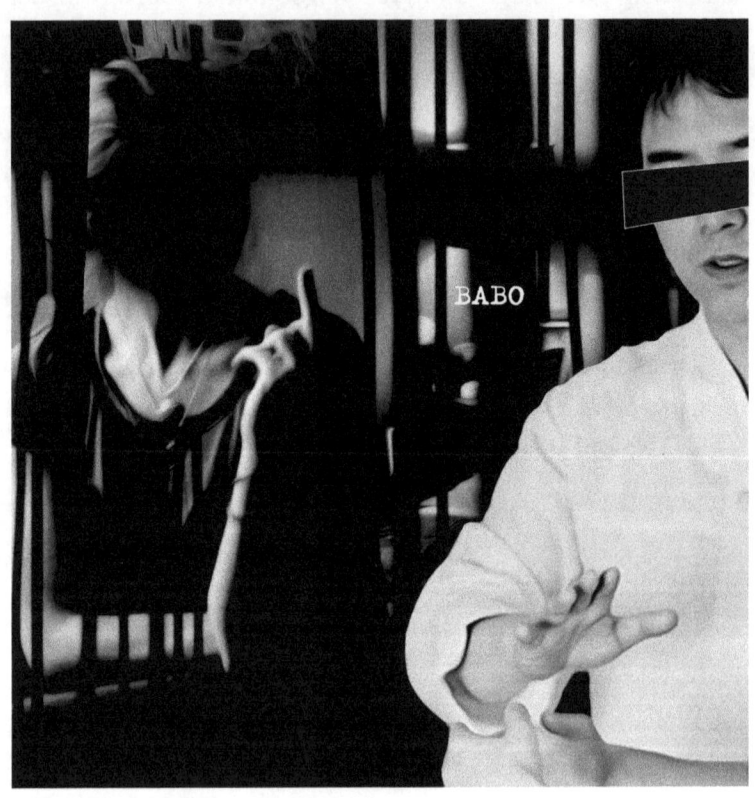

CHAPTER 22

Three Treasures

THREE TREASURES

I

II

these three trees
lie about as good as sahmbo

III

After attending the series of workshops Beescrit Books offered during my first year of involvement, the training to become an official Beescrit instructor was upon me. Something unknown would happen with the 'term' ahead of me and it would be easier to complete. I was bummed. I loved challenges against myself and looked forward to the extreme experience the official instructor training regularly promised. Babo was hesitant to send me and asked if I thought I was ready. I mulled it over for a few days and told Babo I didn't think I was. I wasn't good enough yet. Babo decided to send me anyway and upon completion of my official *'master'* training, I was ceremoniously graced with my own tunic and title.

Daisy took over Paul's position at the bookshop after he had *exited* Beescrit. I was the Assistant Instructor (AI) with Daisy at the same location I had joined as a practitioner. Daisy was the cute one who had tried to help me fit in. I was eventually given Daisy's role and became Lead Instructor selling books, guiding daily Beescrit classes, selling workshops and programs. I felt prepared spiritually, confident I could get my ego out of the way; and *"allow pure cosmic energy, the energy of the True Teacher, and the laws of the universe to flow through me for success."*

Money for *"Beescrit's vision of a more peaceful humanity and healthy Earth"* was the goal. Beescrit told me *"the more connected I was with the True Teacher, the laws of the universe, and Beescrit's vision, the better the financial results would be."* I was twenty-one years old and didn't know business management well. I was successful my first month, but struggled after that. In my fourth month as Lead Instructor a large refund from a Beescrit practitioner pushed my financial starting point back thousands of dollars for several months which suffocated me.

Twenty-one, Lead Instructor, I finished the morning class at the bookshop. I opened the oak-trimmed faux-frosted glass-paned door of the main classroom to find two people in the small bright lobby with matte bamboo floors, a welcoming brownish-gray loveseat, and modern triangular glass-top coffee table; the room divided by a custom oak desk. The two sat on the loveseat. One of them was a practitioner I barely recognized in her street-clothes, but once I identified her, Diane, the other was known to me, though we'd never met. Diane and her friend were dressed to the nines and clearly not happy and very formal about showing it. I was close with Diane and tried like hell to sign her up for an expensive intensive training which seemed to be working wonders for people: Stories of deep depression healed in ten days. Stories of drug addicts getting clean and the paralyzed walking again. I trusted the instructor too, Bernadette.

Diane was not interested in going to Bernadette's training. She told me that she had more money than God—if she tried to spend it all in a lifetime, it would be impossible. I did not understand why Diane did not want to attend Bernadette's training with her wellness goals and boundless dollars. I accepted Diane's decision and moved on to consultations with other people for other workshops and programs. Diane was hurt that she hadn't gotten as much attention or love from me. I admit that I had starkly withdrawn my energy and depth of caring. I hadn't realized how my actions would affect Diane.

Diane's friend dropped a pile of perfectly stacked paperwork onto the oak desk after the other practitioners had left. Diane's friend explained that they knew everything about

Beescrit Books For Wellness, hence the paperwork printed off the internet, likely consisting of cult claims from various sources. Diane and her friend knew their rights and were willing to picket in front of the bookshop if Beescrit didn't refund them virtually every dollar they'd already spent, including their already consumed services. I tried not to show my nervousness. My eyes were fixed on Diane's friend's watch which had been exposed as she put the paperwork on the desk. I tried not to look at the watch but was overwhelmed by it—Diane adorned in jewels, both of them decked out in the finest clothing. It was intimidating; I assume intentionally so. As Diane and her friend threatened Beescrit's business, I found myself standing there in my fancy pajamas thinking, *they have no idea I am twenty-one years old and have absolutely no clue what I am doing.*

After Diane's visit, I felt guilty for withdrawing in the way I had with her. I meant Diane no harm and didn't realize Diane cared about me enough that I had the ability to hurt her at all. In retrospect, it is obvious Diane cared about me, but at the time I thought I was garbage and it was only PCE that gave me value. Realizing the harm I had unintentionally caused her, I committed myself to a resolution from that moment on: I would love every single person I met, equally and unconditionally, without looking for anything in return. I later randomly encountered Diane in the grocery store in town. We both paused but said nothing. I remember Diane's eyes and I don't think she was mad. It was a meeting of two tortured souls, vulnerably and silently viewing one another.

Hi, Diane, I am not sure I ever did get the chance to apologize properly. I am sorry...

So very Sorry.

I was completely fucked business-management-wise in the wake of Diane's refund. I loved the people I met and I liked loving people. Some people were harder to figure out how to love than others, some preferred space and respect, others liked hugs. Most everyone was comfortable with a smile.

My experience with Diane taught me that human beings need not just pure cosmic energy, but steady care and attention. I discovered all people needed pure cosmic energy equally, no matter if they brought a buck or not. I tried *"being PCE as much as possible with everyone and even alone, without expectations, because my spiritual growth wasn't just for me; it was for Jack, Owen, Oskar, my grandparents, Grace, for every animal and plant, it was for the Earth and humanity."*

No matter how hard I tried, the cash did not flow at the bookshop. What did this mean? I must have connected with PCE using too much of my own willingness. How am I supposed to get the hell out of the way? Long story short, I sucked at it. People liked me, but I couldn't make enough money. Babo was actively coaching me at the time, that dumb piece of shit, fancying himself his own version of a CEO. I still couldn't do it though, even cutting the spiritual line to connect with PCE and the True Teacher through my closest available conduit, Babo, so graciously guiding me and sacrificing himself.

If Beescrit's philosophical precepts were correct I should have excelled to the extreme. I should have made money with ease in the material world under Beescrit's guidelines. If money didn't flow to a bookshop, a Lead Instructor must be impeding the money or lacking spiritual connection.

Beescrit Books harbors three treasures which are: *"The True Teacher, Beescrit's goal, and the laws of the universe. All three treasures are interchangeable. Laws of the universe equals True Teacher. The True Teacher embodies Beescrit's goal. Beescrit's goal is a sacred tool bestowed by the True Teacher upon his students in order for them to become one with him spiritually and therefore one with the laws of the universe. All connected.*" This is the crux of Beescrit Books For Wellness. Within Beescrit Books, these three "treasures" are deeply sacred.

"If you were not making enough money you were likely not connected enough to Sahmbo, the three treasures. If you called PCE in your mind as much as you could, your chances of being connected with the three treasures would be great."

Yeah, yeah, yeah! Hogwash and bullshit! I can say this now, but back then I was already an expert at erasing myself. My excommunicated ego could neither conjure the sentiments nor express the words. *Beescrit gee-doe-jahs, are you aghast?*

CHAPTER 23

Cotton, RD

BEESCRIT GEE-DOE-JAH / CHLOE

Beescrit's practices for wellness are highly effective in normal doses and, like most things, harmful taken to excess. Three hundred Beescrit instructors gathered at the meditation retreat center in the desert for the company's annual meeting. Surrounded by beauty, smiling faces, and a buffet of healthy foods, we attended a smorgasbord of spiritual training and lectures. We spent an afternoon with Bernadette who shared her money-making secrets in the dollop hall.

Bernadette's practice was familiar but more intense. Bernadette stood in front of the group and announced that we would be hitting ourselves for three hours straight. Everyone laughed but I knew Bernadette was serious. Bernadette started us off at a regular pace, beginning by gently having us bounce up and down while tapping our entire body with our palms.

Several minutes passed, then Bernadette stopped us and asked, "Where is your mind?"

Everyone chuckled because we knew our minds were not necessarily in our bodies. Bernadette asked how we thought we could do the exercise to more effectively bring the mind to the present.

I singularly called out, "Do it harder!"

Bernadette confirmed that was exactly it; "Harder, faster, and even harder where it hurts!"

Eventually Bernadette guided us to add the use of our voices. We could call out anything at all, stream-of-consciousness, just as long as we didn't stop talking. "I hate this;" or "This hurts;" were acceptable. Fast, loud, and intense instrumental music shook the hall. I always hoped the next training would be the training that freed me, the one rendering me enlightened, perfect, and a natural delight. We did the hitting and talking and yelling exercise for three hours straight. I went to the bathroom afterwards and saw the insides of my thighs completely bruised. Beescrit says *"bruising caused by practices is stagnant blood and energy leaving the body."* I don't think this is completely wrong—*gua sha* can cause bruising, as does cupping. It might not be terrible to do the intensive hitting for ten days. People were getting incredible results practicing with Bernadette. For instructors though, this extreme style of practice does not stop after ten days. The practices are integrated into daily life. Whatever was required to get the ego out of the way and allow pure cosmic energy to suck in the denaro, must be done.

"Why?"

"For Beescrit's goal of peace on Earth and in the hearts of mankind!"

"Why does Beescrit need all that money?"

"For the True Teacher to spread the word and gain the respect of society!"

"And also to plan effectively for when the sea rises and land becomes oceans by purchasing properties which will remain above sea level so we could all live there," and finally, *"to pay for all business expenses including everyone's salary."*

There was talk of instructors getting stock in the company or individual bank accounts with a certain amount of money for each of them.

...wonder if any of that is set up yet?

Babo was removed from our region of Beescrit bookshop locations shortly after returning from the annual meeting featuring Bernadette's money-maker program experience. I am almost certain Babo crossed the line with a practitioner and his manipulative promiscuity was discovered, so he had to be moved. I succeeded as Lead Instructor after Babo was gone, making $30K three months in a row for Beescrit Books from my small location of around fifty practitioners registered for daily class memberships. I could not have done it without help. A Half Commitment Instructor, Harper HCI, arrived unexpectedly from California to help sell books, teach daily classes, and deliver flyers for the bookshop. Harper made molletas for lunch and introduced me to a perfectly delicious chilled dessert of ripe bananas in condensed milk with cinnamon on top.

Hello my dear friend, I love you so much! You and your sweet children made my life rosier back then; and you have remained my good friend all these years, even though we live a world apart. Thanks for always being there.

I had made an agreement with Babo to keep quiet. In hindsight, I considered the terms of my silence with him an asset because they caused me confusion which in turn lended itself to doubt. On a private walk, Babo had taken me around our neighborhood before he would leave the region and Cotton would replace him. Babo alluded vaguely to our sexual encounters on the walk.

Babo asked me, "Why did we do that?"

I said, *"To deepen my connection with True Nature and grow my soul faster."*

Babo said, "No. It was because we were in love."

Is that what he thought? If so, we had a great misunderstanding. Babo told me to always deny it, to anyone, because our situation could be easily misperceived. I was hesitant to agree to this because I worried if the True Teacher asked me about it. Was I to lie to Itchee too? I asked Babo about my conundrum. He said I should absolutely lie to the True Teacher. *WOW!*

I found this very strange and frankly stupid of Babo: *"Doesn't the True Teacher know everything? Or if he doesn't know it, can Itchee not perceive truth somehow with his enlightenment and clarity?"*

I thought part of Beescrit's shtick was that of a largely infallible and all-knowing True Teacher. Stories circulated about phenomenal things the True Teacher had done, for example, extinguishing an impressive amount of candles on a birthday cake with a hand motion and the powers of energy. My agreement with Babo did not add up; but, whatever... I agreed to stay quiet. The agreement was immensely confusing, but I took my promise seriously.

In Beescrit, *"the word of your Regional Director is as good as the word of the True Teacher himself."* That is the hierarchy. Concerning anyone above another member in rank, *his word is THE word.* As a gee-doe-jah, it was unsafe to question authority or those senior in years of service in Beescrit. This varied depending on individual temperaments. Two individuals specifically come to my mind: Chloe, a woman with short dark hair with a ruddy tint and a uniquely beautiful jawline, and a man named Jamie. Jamie was above both Chloe and me in hierarchical status but was one of the most humble and kind, in sharp contrast to Chloe's overall boisterous manner and dramatic expressions. Having entered into Beescrit at a young age, Chloe technically held seniority, even to those older than herself in age.

Chloe, you always made me laugh even though you were such a bitch to everyone. I liked you because you were bitchy and whiny which I found endearing and authentic. I mostly loved working with you as your Assistant Instructor. I wish I could see your face when you read this. Your cheeks will flush with embarrassment as you get the attention you naturally command and deserve. Yes, you do fucking matter. From what you told me, Chloe, it seems your uncertainty stems from the undefined and unattainable standards of excellence your mother required of you. Your mother imposed a standard of beauty upon you, which is honestly ridiculous that she didn't find you pretty enough. As an expert in this area, Chloe, I speak to your mother on your behalf here: "Fuck off! You are missing out on your beautiful daughter." I think you would love the real world so much, Chloe. You'd be like a kid in a candy store, even now that you consider yourself an old hag.

There was a new Regional Director named Cotton. The name Cotton was bestowed upon her by the True Teacher because she was comforting like cotton. Cotton was a seasoned and favorite instructor in Beescrit. She took me under her wing after Babo had gotten the boot. Babo was still around though, and I had to be in the same room with him sometimes until he finally disappeared from Beescrit entirely.

We moved to a new house.

"Too many ghosts at the other house," Cotton said.

Cotton, the new RD, spent an enormous amount of time with me. We got close. I took up the task of cleaning Cotton's room as I had done when Babo was in the role of Regional Director. On the last day of the month, during my short stint of success working with Harper HCI as Lead Instructor at the first bookshop I had managed, I carefully watched the income and expenses on the company's computer system, BRBnet, to be sure

I had made a net profit, not only having accrued my financial goal. I had questions because the numbers did not add up. My location's income far exceeded its expenses at this time. When I entered income into Beescrit's BRBnet system, a disproportionate chunk went right to expenses, reducing or barely affecting net profit. I suppose the numbers could work out that way, technically, if one were to look at the company and its affiliates as one entity, instead of as individual locations and companies.

Cotton was proud of what I was accomplishing. $30K from a small location was above average. In the burst of confidence I gained from my success, eating spicy ramen together at the kitchen table, I asked Cotton about the numbers that didn't make sense to me. Cotton was pissed. She told me it was everyone's salary, the rent of all the locations, the taxes and maintenance for properties purchased for Beescrit Books For Wellness, and a percentage that went straight to the True Teacher's consulting company. I got the silent treatment for about a week until Cotton finally spoke to me one evening. I was coming out of the kitchen and she was in the hall. We met for a moment at the top of the stairs. Cotton asked me why I had asked such a question about the numbers and income when she had not thought of it herself in twenty years of service. Realizing I may have stirred up Cotton's perspective on her life decisions, I politely said I did not know and then apologized for having asked it.

I proceeded to fail after that. And not slightly. Most Lead Instructors could make $13K or $15K; mostly upwards of $18K per month at one location. Some locations regularly contributed $30K or more in one month; yes, from a bookshop. I was hovering around the $3K to $8K range. I could not stay at the Beescrit location working with Harper HCI no matter how much Cotton would've liked me to. I accepted my defeat and decided to happily support one of the larger locations in the subservient role of Assistant Instructor. I needed to work on my humility anyway. It would be good for me, I thought.

Beescrit and Cotton tossed me around from location to location which was a superb practice in non-attachment. I settled nowhere. The Lead Instructor at one of the locations I was working at, Bob, got called away to a training in the desert. Bob left me in charge. Cotton frequently checked in on me via phone calls. I happily took on responsibility for all work at the location for those four days that Bob was away. Cotton called the day before Bob was scheduled to return. She asked how I was going to make all the money for the location. I told her I was responsible only for the money I said I would make while Bob was away, towards my regular monthly goal, and it was going great! Cotton told me Bob was not coming back.

"You can do it," Cotton said.

I did not want the promotion. I pissed and moaned a little, and Cotton obliged, but I knew it had already been decided.

CHAPTER 24

Oops!

By Thanksgiving 2008, I had taken over Bob's role as Lead Instructor at the bookshop which was not far from Grace's house. I had been involved with Beescrit Books for just over four years by this time and the major lawsuit had been filed against the organization in this same year. My parents had divorced in 2004 and I had since visited both of them on holidays, one in the morning, one in the evening. In 2008, I decided I wanted to visit only one parent per holiday. Oskar was fine with the new arrangement. Grace kicked and screamed. I told Oskar plans had changed because Grace was crying about Thanksgiving being *her holiday,* which it was not. There were zero stipulations in place for holidays, the topic had never been discussed. I did not want Grace to feel sad and Oskar understood this, so I changed my plans and told Grace I would be at her house for Thanksgiving dinner. Grace's tears dried up, but now she was somewhat defiant. Grace told me I could come to her house, but she wouldn't be there.

"Okay, Mom, fine," but I assured her that I would be coming to visit anyway.

I knew there was a good chance Grace wouldn't be at her house when I arrived, and she was not, but the front door was unlocked so I went in. Just in case Grace pulled a no-show, I had come equipped with cleaning supplies to busy myself until she'd come back. I sent Grace a text message letting her know I was at the house; she let me know she was at a motel with no intention of showing up.

The house was a fucking mess. When I finally made my way upstairs and entered Grace's room I fell to my knees and cried. I was so sad that my mother was living like this. Gathering myself, I wiped the tears off my face and sucked the snot back up into my head with a sniff. I stood, determined to make it better. First, I tore the linens off the bed and brought them to the basement to throw them in the washing machine. I averted my eyes, keeping my attention on the task at hand, for I couldn't bear the sight of boxed memories ruined by the flood in the basement. I cleaned most of the rooms, excluding my brother Owen's room and his bathroom. I spent seven hours cleaning and Grace was still not home, so I left. Not long after, I got a phone call from Grace. She was pleased I had cleaned the house and thanked me in a loving and kind tone, which informed me that I had succeeded in making her feel cared about. I simply told Grace she was welcome. About three minutes later Grace called again, this time, crying.

"You cleaned the upstairs too," Grace said.

I confirmed that yes, I had, then I heard Owen in the background.

He was calling out to me jokingly, loud enough so I could hear through the phone, "Hey! Why didn't you clean my room too?"

I chuckled politely and that was done. Then I drank a six pack of beer.

I made the best of my role as Lead Instructor as usual. I most enjoyed my time working at Beescrit Books when practitioners came around for daily self-help practice sessions, even when I didn't feel like standing in front of them to deliver wellness techniques and pure cosmic energy. I worked alone. It was winter and the lawsuit was underway. The money started slowing down. I arrived for a nighttime business meeting. Cotton was in the private office at the bookshop and called me in. I knew it wasn't a personal call because Cotton had a translator at the ready. She and I communicated just fine even though we didn't speak the same language most of the time. We were close, and I think it was obvious we cared about each other, yet I had a hard time consistently trusting those above me in the hierarchy after my experience with Babo. Doubt in the hierarchy strained my relationship with Cotton along with my inability to bring home the bacon. Some part of me clung to what little was left of me, and I reflected that *that was exactly my problem.*

It was Cotton's job to make sure all of us did what we were supposed to and achieved our financial goals for the bookshops in the region. Cotton motioned me to sit across from her at a small table in the office. I started eating a snack off the table and was happy to be in her company. I loved her. The translator sat with us and I put my hands in my lap, straightening my back.

Cotton looked me square in the eyes and said in her native tongue, "Vada, when are you going to overcome yourself and achieve your business goals?"

I told Cotton, "I don't know."

"When are you going to wake up, Vada?" Cotton asked me through the translator.

I responded that I was trying desperately but for some reason could not do it.

Then she asked, "Why aren't you drawing in business by using PCE practices?"

Before I could respond; Cotton asserted firmly that if it weren't illegal, she would slap me, but because it was illegal, I should do it for myself.

"How?" I asked.

Cotton told me to start and I did so without hesitation. I smacked my cheeks repeatedly as hard as I could, alternating hands with each strike. I kept my eyes closed but stopped for a moment and asked how long I should do it.

Cotton said in English, "Until you wake up."

I struck my face and head for I do not know how long, wishing to be enlightened or something so I could finally stop being such a goddamn burden. She eventually stopped me and ordered me to keep my eyes closed. It is no surprise at this point that I followed Cotton's instructions.

Cotton spoke and the translator followed, "Who told you to hit your eyes?"

Surprised, I asked, "Did I hit my eyes?"

"Yes."

Cotton spoke again and I understood some of what she said in her language—something about an egg. My eyes still closed, I heard the translator open the refrigerator, then I held the egg she placed in my right hand.

Cotton said through the translator, "Roll the egg over your eye."

"Which one?" I asked.

"Both," they said in unison.

At this, I tried opening my eyes. The right eye didn't open at all, the left opened about halfway. *Oops!*

Oops! Seriously, that's what I thought. The reality was not good and by morning it was worse. I hid from Cotton several days afterwards and she definitely did not want to see me. I knew I should spare her the atrocity. I was several shades of purple, looking like some strange lumpy underground sewer monster. I did my best to cover it with makeup. Nobody noticed mostly, though I am not sure how because my face was so swollen. One person, however, did notice. A new practitioner named Betty, a dark-haired and fair-skinned professional actor with delicate features, arrived early for the regular morning session. She asked about the condition of my face. I assured Betty I was fine. I told her that I had slipped on some ice and provided a simple yet detailed account of the whole thing. Betty was still worried that something was not right with my head. *More than she could ever know!* Betty sat me down and phoned her children's pediatrician. I was mortified but went along with it, even got on the phone with the doctor to whom I told the exact same story as I'd just told Betty. The doctor asked if I had a headache, double-vision, things of that nature. I said no, which was true. The doctor reassured the beautiful Betty that I seemed fine.

I carried on as usual with Beescritspeak running through my battered head: *"I still needed to make the money. Compared to the current suffering of humanity and the wretched state of the Earth, my suffering was small. The giant island of plastic floating in our ocean right now—my suffering was not as pressing as that now was it? The goal was always bigger. Literally always foremost, as a rule the goal was king, for humanity and for the Earth."*

Within a few days the swelling subsided and the color evened out enough that minimal makeup did the trick to normalize my skin tone. I was dying inside when Cotton shipped me off to work in the city that never sleeps. I do not know where I actually resided at this time. It was definitely in one of two states; I guess wherever I paid the rent. I liked the city. No one knew me and I could hide in plain sight without concern. I showered at the gym across the street from the bookshop. The gym had a sauna and someone else cleaned it. Now how can anybody complain about that!? I even felt free enough to smoke a cigarette, standing just out of sight where someone else had probably just peed. Sure smelled like it. But Wowza! That was life! With any luck, I would come upon an abandoned building with an available front stoop to comfortably claim as my own for ten minutes, pretending to be autonomous. My time in the big city lasted eight weeks. The woman I worked under at the location was very kind and took care of me. She barely made me do any work, so I didn't mind the little I had to do. Plus, the freedom of the city—it was cake. We ate out, ordered in, or cooked on a small propane burner we had set atop the toilet seat. The regional communal house required subway travel and then a walk through a tough area, so we mostly slept at the bookshop.

Meanwhile, there were other plans for me. Cotton was moved to a large region of bookshops in the state of New York, in areas outside of Manhattan, where she would fulfill her duties as Regional Director. After working eight weeks in the big city, Cotton called me to live and work under her in the new region. Once there, I took care of her, cleaned her room, treated her well, and served her tea in the evenings at home. Cotton's stress was abundant. Her financial responsibility was cumulative of all locations in the region, and this was a big region. If one bookshop made less money, the others had to make up the difference, and Cotton was responsible for making sure it happened. With more responsibility, gee-doe-jahs had slightly more freedom in Beescrit. I was happy being the low man on the totem pole, serving everybody else. Less freedom but also less stress. There was this dynamic demand of month-to-month high-pressured financial goals. Beescrit played unethical games in regions to achieve these objectives. I trust these schemes were most likely illegal. If the ample chargebacks and refunds of the company were put through a review, they would certainly throw up a red flag. Beescrit accountants started catching on by the time I left them in 2013. The ends don't typically justify the means. It is the Beescrit instructors, HCIs, and practitioners who muddle with the money games; Itchee-Ree does not. It never sat right with me.

Why does the True Teacher live a lavish lifestyle while instructors practically panhandle for money, not even for themselves, but for the vision? Yes, the True Teacher needs money to spread the word in style so Itchee can be respected; but excuse this guy for his lavish spending!? Is that at all justifiable? I am not even talking about the Hummer Itchee reportedly drove. Peace on Earth is what we worked for, frazzled and sweating. We would benefit greatly in the life beyond, in oneness with all. Thanks so much, Itchee. So much gratitude! Surely you enjoy your life, living off your slave labor.

CHAPTER 25

Eleanor

The lawsuit hovered over Beescrit for more than three years, starting in 2008. By 2009 I was working with Cotton in the state of New York, and the True Teacher somehow procured a famous venue for a show starring himself. I think it was an effort for Beescrit to save face. I practiced martial arts and a type of drumming for the show. It was quite the experience being on that stage. Once in a lifetime. It was a huge venue and the event didn't come close to filling up the house, despite our best efforts to promote ticket sales through the bookshops. *Could it have been due to half the bookshop locations closing and an exodus of Koreans returning to their country to dodge lawsuit charges?*

Grace showed up at the venue. This is the only time Grace visited me after she'd attended Beescrit classes and workshops during my first year of practice at Beescrit Books. Grace wore a long white linen dress with tasteful muted flowers, but what I remember most is the person Grace was with when I found her after the show—that fucking shit-for-brains Babo! Grace and Babo had been seated next to each other. I couldn't freakin' believe my own two formerly-battered eyes! What are the odds? Grace and Babo were chummy standing side by side in the lobby. *I wanted to barf...on both of them...spewingly and grotesquely...I'm talkin' Exorcist-style here...but I was frozen stiff.* Afterwards I distracted myself by volunteering to scour the city for cellophane to wrap a flower arrangement.

In Cotton's new region, I moved back and forth between two houses, depending on my schedule, location-hopping as an Assistant Instructor. Whichever Lead Instructor needed help on a particular day, I went to her bookshop. By the end of 2009, I worked full-time with a Lead Instructor named Eleanor. I liked Eleanor and still do, though we are estranged. English is

Eleanor's first language which was quite a delight. Eleanor's initial identified task was removing the strange accent I'd acquired by using broken English for approximately five years. People often speculated I was from the Netherlands.

I made a fair amount of money for Beescrit under Eleanor, but did not receive the credit, which was how I liked it. I did want to grow spiritually in the material world, helping people in real time in real life, but it was too nerve-racking to get the recognition. Working with Eleanor, my anxiety reduced to achieve goals and I began attaining them with ease. I set a goal for $5K one month and reached it. Next I tried for $10K, reached that one too. Next I tried just $12K because $10K already seemed high enough. The month I tried for $12K, I ka-chinged $24K at the location. Eleanor was obviously happy and I was happier working with Eleanor just behind the scenes. I felt more real somehow, maybe relative to losing the accent?

Eleanor and I prepared to eat lunch one afternoon in a small private room with high ceilings. The sun cozied the space through paper screens covering the windows. We sat cross-legged on the floor at a short table as we ate and chatted. Word had gotten around that Babo had been *exited* from Beescrit. Without any rhyme or reason, I spilled my guts out with the story of my sexual relationship with Babo. I didn't even know it was surfacing from my inner self, much less from my stomach. Eleanor immediately started crying; then she moved herself around back of me, wrapped her legs and arms around me, and rocked me. Eleanor cried; I did not. I remember thinking, *Wait, maybe this wasn't my fault?* I had thought that I had been guilty of creating the situation. Moreover, I thought I had chosen it.

Eleanor explained that what Babo had done to me was unequivocally wrong.

Eleanor sent me a text message recently. I have not replied. Eleanor, this is my response to you now: *I wish the story of our friendship was different too. You are a force of good, my friend. You have bled in Beescrit for nearly two decades; surrendering your heart, your soul, and your time. You are an activist, your son at the core of your activism. You told me you wanted a better world for him. You thought Beescrit Books was the answer. It was my answer. September 11th was still fresh when you found yourself pregnant with him and happened upon a holistic bookshop where you would, against-all-odds, dedicate your life for a better world and be a mother. I think you consistently succeed in Beescrit because of your love for your family. If you do not succeed financially in Beescrit, you will be shipped away from your family like everyone else. We are not much different from our mammalian counterparts socially. We need each other. Beescrit speaks of healing families, but their actions do not match the sentiment. Beescrit tends to break families apart in the name of spiritual growth, don't you think? I am sorry to tell you this, but I cannot be silent. I love you always.*

After Eleanor was done crying and consoling me— sweetheart and love-powerhouse that she truly is—I felt mildly okay. *Perhaps consoled by a cleaner conscience?* We finished lunch. An hour or so later, a remorse like slow warm molasses smothered me. I had broken my promise of silence, unforgivable. There was a new feeling though and a new thought lurking in my soul: *Maybe, just maybe, Babo did do something bad, and I was neither the cause nor the culprit in it. Maybe this exonerated me from breaking my promise of silence too. Perhaps I was even duty-bound to speak.*

Because of Eleanor's emotional response regarding Babo's actions, I thought it was a good idea to let Cotton know what had happened to me with Babo. Maybe my encounters with Babo were the root of why I struggled with trusting Cotton. I was surprised when Cotton got angry at me.

Cotton said, clearly agitated in English with a heavy accent, "Why did you tell that information to Eleanor? Do you think that is good for her spiritual growth?"

Hmmm, weird response. She continued, telling me she had assumed Babo was abusing me. I had been working with Cotton for four years by this time and she had never mentioned it, not a whisper, and she'd had ample opportunity.

I was preoccupied with daily tasks like handing out flyers and teaching classes, calling pure cosmic energy, and doing private sessions. Women came to Beescrit for fertility and baby-wise, I was two for two *"through the highly effective Beescrit practices for wellness."* A woman with multiple sclerosis eventually walked without aid, besides braces on her calves and ankles, and started sitting up from laying down on the floor by herself. It was amazing! More commonly, practices resolved chronic back pain, digestive issues, and promoted overall wellbeing for the body and mind. A participant could progress to the next level with workshops. Maybe one day even become an instructor! *Hahaha! No, really.*

I became Acting Lead Instructor after working steadily at Eleanor's bookshop for about two years. Eleanor got promoted, but I failed again. As long as my name was not associated with profits I was okay making money, but as soon as my name was linked to the dollar amount on BRBnet, I couldn't do it. Anxiety would overtake me and I couldn't access my authenticity or think clearly. I moved locations again, almost became Lead Instructor at the new spot because of an instructor's visa issue, but then I moved once more and landed in The Bronx.

CHAPTER 26

The Bronx

I moved back to the house in Queens with Cotton because it was the closest commute to my new bookshop location, and I ultimately took refuge in the Bronx. My transfer to the Bronx marked my eighth year of service at Beescrit Books.

Practitioners in the Bronx were ardent lovers of life. With direct, mostly loud, clear, accented speech, the toughest individuals were kinder than Mother Theresa. Paradoxically, the externally tough characters softened my stiff heart. One young woman, Angel HCI, loved me from the moment she laid eyes on me solely because I was the new Lead Instructor. Angel was a nurse who stood four feet ten inches tall with dark hair and eyes. Angel HCI greeted me by name and proper title, and hugged me enthusiastically. She held on in hugs longer than I was comfortable, sometimes telling me she loved me. The first time Angel told me she loved me was when my rigid heart began adjusting to warmth. *Angel, you had dreamed of a family of your own and I am happy that came true for you! I am forever grateful to you, Angel. I'd guess you don't know how much you helped me let love into my heart, albeit uncomfortably at first. I had grown cold.* I felt that the practitioners took care of me in the Bronx more than I did them.

The Bronx was rough around the edges but with a supremely tolerant community of people. People in the area had an awareness of themselves and the fact that they resided among assorted cultures. From their hearts, they hoped to be accepted as much as they accepted others; regardless of race, creed, age, economic status, or lifestyle. Aware of the possibility they might get stabbed in the back, most of them chose to be nice anyway, to anybody—the kind of people who would literally give you the shirt off their backs.

Hurricane Sandy swept through the borough and knocked the power out for several weeks, but the shower in the Bronx Beescrit Books location still functioned as usual, and the cockroaches stayed off the countertops in the kitchen during the day. They were tiny cockroaches but cockroaches nonetheless. I cleaned up the dead ones in drawers and cabinets, and caulked holes around the countertops, but they still came. I accepted them as part of the territory. Thank goodness they were so small because there were a lot of them. There was also a gas shortage in the area because of hurricane damages. This gave me relief with the excuse not to return home, "reserving my gas" and staying safe in the Bronx among people by whom I felt loved.

Can't lie, I was at my wits' end with the financial monthly goals of Beescrit Books For Wellness. I just wanted to love people and I thought that was the whole point, so that is what I did. The bookshop was moderately successful.

Esther HCI worked at a theater and taught part-time at the bookshop. The train was up and running before the gas supply evened out, and Esther asked if I wanted a ticket to see the Philharmonic Orchestra. I walked to the train station and headed into the city. The orchestra enlivened my brain, drenching it in auditory and visual delight. I stared, soaking it up, tears silently streaming. The concert opened a window to the wonders of real life for me once again. I had been removed and sheltered from it for so long. *Thank you, Esther.*

I met another young woman in the Bronx by springtime, a new practitioner named Aphrodite. I loved her just the same as everyone else. Aphrodite came to group sessions semi-regularly, and did ten private sessions with me. She told me she was sick, which she was, but she did not appear to be sick. I found Aphrodite beautiful, as I did most people. I corresponded with Aphrodite via email regarding private session schedule changes, but Aphrodite suggested we start using text messages instead.

It was the last day of the month and Aphrodite was supposed to come to the bookshop for a private self-help session, but texted me saying she wasn't feeling well enough to come. I was thinking she might renew her private session package, which would help me achieve the monthly financial goal at the bookshop. Aphrodite asked if I would visit her at her home and I said yes. Each time I arrived at Aphrodite's apartment door, face to face with the brownish-gray paint and fish-eye peephole, I thought to myself, *Vada, what the fuck are you doing here?* Aphrodite welcomed me, as did her fluffy dog. She sat on the couch and I, on a chair. After regular niceties, because I had to get back to the bookshop and figure out how the heck I was going to generate $10K out of thin air within a couple of hours, I asked Aphrodite directly if she planned to renew her private session package. She got emotional, saying she felt unsupported by her family, and her medical bills were too much. I completely understood. I never liked pressing anyone to sign up for things, and I did not want people's money if they did not want to give it.

Aphrodite coaxed me onto the couch with her. I moved over there, but stayed all the way on the opposite side. She was about my age and started crushing on me before I realized it. Aphrodite thought I liked her too because I was so caring with her, but I knew I was just the same with everyone. She had a blanket over her legs, looking quite comfortable on the couch. She gazed at me. *Lesbians, some know the look, as if my womanly object was some sort of delicious ice cream cone or something. Loaded with attraction and magnetism, Aphrodite's eyes swallowed me whole.*

Aphrodite asked me, "Is there anything you want to tell me?"

Mother fucker, what the fuck; I was sucked in by her eye tractor beams. What the hell was happening and why were my body and brain responding in such an uncharacteristic manner? My personal desires were stirred for a second. My eyeballs were probably gauged out of my head. It was Easter Sunday and I had gotten Aphrodite an adorable chick-shaped cupcake from one of my favorite bakeries. I nervously excused myself and reminded her to enjoy the cupcake.

Aphrodite texted me after I returned to the bookshop, apologizing that she could not support my work by re-registering for private sessions. It was fine. I really didn't care about the money, and I told Aphrodite so. It didn't matter if she registered or not. I had a long way to go and not a lot of time to produce many dollars. The last day of the month in Beescrit is the pits, second only to the first several days of the following month which are spent tying up the accounting from the previous month. Meanwhile, Aphrodite and I chatted back and forth, a welcomed distraction from my reality. She told me if I wanted to let her know about anything else, she was open to it. I knew exactly what Aphrodite meant, but we both communicated cryptically. I told her I would let her know my thoughts on the proposition, if I had any.

Aphrodite worried me intensely; she was often expressing a lack of willingness to live because of her disease and threatening to stop taking her medications. When the True

Teacher's side-kick Daniel visited the Beescrit residence to see Cotton, I asked him about the situation with Aphrodite. Daniel told me that if Aphrodite were terminally ill, which technically she was, I should make her comfortable. I prayed and meditated for many hours trying to figure out what I should do for Aphrodite, simultaneously considering trying a same-sex relationship and how I personally felt about that. I was supposed to be willing to do *anything* for Beescrit's vision.

For Beescrit's vision, I decided to try a relationship with Aphrodite. I was weary and unsure how I could realistically grow an intimate interpersonal relationship considering my responsibilities and workload at the bookshop, night training, and meetings. I could be called at a moment's notice and expected to be somewhere. First I told Aphrodite yes, I would try a relationship with her. The same day I realized just how unrealistic it was. I would never be able to be in an intimate relationship with anyone. I messaged Aphrodite immediately after finishing my work at the bookshop and asked if I could come over. She consented and before I knew it, I stood in front of the fisheye peephole in the dark narrow hallway, knowing I had no business in that place. I told Aphrodite that, although I cared for her deeply, I could never be whom she wanted in a romantic relationship. Aphrodite was coy and didn't really respond. She just looked at me with her huge dark eyes. I was awkward as hell. Eventually Aphrodite excused herself to the bathroom. As Aphrodite walked past me her scent of vanilla and lavender messed with my head something ferocious. I turned around to see her walking into the bathroom and noticed her thick dark hair perfectly blown out, cut to a length a little less than halfway down her back. I was so confused. I turned back in my seat, closed my eyes, straightened my back, and pleaded with my heart to please tell me what to do.

My heart said: "Kiss her when she comes back."

Before leaning in, I looked at Aphrodite and asked, "Are you ready?" Real smooth. We kissed and it was like a fireworks finale in my brain. I thought to myself, *My god, is this what kissing is supposed to feel like?*

I was excited. Aphrodite and I texted during the daytime and planned to watch a movie and have a sleepover on the weekend. It worked out perfectly with Cotton attending a Regional Directors meeting out of town.

By the time I arrived at Aphrodite's apartment that weekend, I had again concluded it was not fair of me to try and have a relationship with her or anyone. I stared at the fisheye peephole as the dog announced my arrival before I lifted my knuckles to knock. I told Aphrodite again I was very sorry, but I did not think I was the person she was looking for. We sat excruciatingly far away from each other on the couch, watching a movie. I found myself open to an intimate relationship, wanting it even. I slept over Aphrodite's apartment but nothing happened. I was losing weight under the stress of the situation, coupled with the rest of my usual responsibilities and schedule. I was a mess.

I left Aphrodite's apartment under weird circumstances, having just slept over without any communication about how I thought we could not continue. Aphrodite was relatively mean and she warned me she would hurt me in the end. Our entire relationship lasted ten days. I had been in longer relationships before, but in none of them did my heart ever break. This heartbreak cracked a gaping hole in my chest which could not be soothed, no matter how I positioned myself. *Damn, that shit really hurt!* I couldn't sleep. Morning finally came. I coaxed myself up for a shower after rolling back and forth on the floor where I had tried to sleep the previous night, and where I slept any night I could avoid going home. I walked across the bright yellow vinyl flooring of the spiritual classroom in socked feet, through the kitchen past my cockroach friends, and into the bathroom for a shower. I got a text message from Aphrodite asking if I would come over to her place for a proper good-bye. I agreed to go there. It was not pleasant, but it was not awful. After some days, the pain in my heat lightened its grip. I was disappointed in how I had handled myself, but prepared to move on, back to the way it was.

APHRODITE

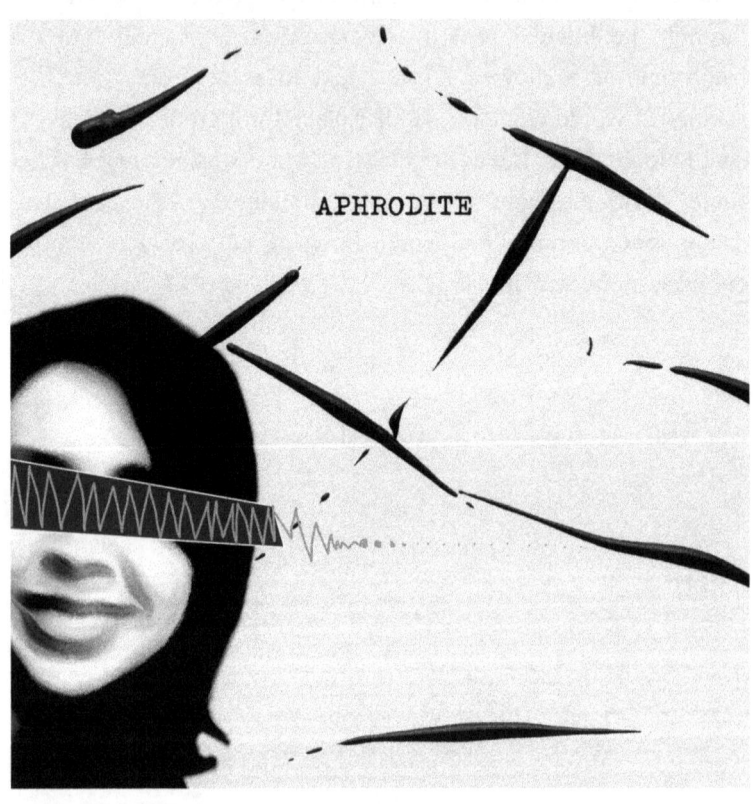

CHAPTER 27

With A Woman

The Bronx Beescrit Books For Wellness hosted a regional workshop one Sunday in April 2012, just weeks after Vada and Aphrodite had come to an end. I assisted the visiting instructor and prepared snacks for practitioners. During the workshop I got an email from the human resource department regarding a complaint submitted by Aphrodite for emotional distress. I was embarrassed: Beescrit had just tied a bow on that major legal mess from 2008 and here I was, Vada, potentially creating another. I found the visiting instructor for the workshop in the private room I had prepared for him. An incredibly nice guy, and many years my senior in Beescrit, I went to Jamie for help. He chose the name *Jamie* because his Korean name was too difficult for English-speakers. Many instructors selected English names. I knocked on the door and Jamie light-heartedly called me in.

He looked at me and asked, "What happened?"

I explained I had done something awful. Jamie, noticing my seriousness, jokingly asked if I'd killed someone.

"No, but it's still pretty bad."

"Did you have a relationship with a practitioner?"

"Yes, but it's worse than that."

"How…'worse'?"

"It was with a woman."

Jamie told me he already knew I liked women. I was astonished! *How!? How did he know my secret that I wasn't privy to myself?*

"How could you tell that, Jamie?"

"By the way you treat men more like they're your brothers."

"Maybe I'm bisexual?" I asked without assurance.

"I do not think you're bisexual, and I'm pretty confident about that... Don't worry about it too much, okay?"

This made me chuckle, but I was very worried.

I called Oskar, outing myself for the potential trouble I had made at work regarding my gayness. I was afraid Beescrit might kick me out, or suffer badly because of my choices, and I would have no option but to *exit* Beescrit. Oskar said he didn't know what to say about the sexuality piece, but told me he had a couch I could sleep on if I ended up needing to. I also spoke with the legal department at Beescrit Books whose representative told me the situation was more common than I might think and not to worry, which surprised me. Oskar sent me a text message the morning after we spoke to let me know he had done a Google search. From what he could tell, it seemed sexuality could be fluid throughout a person's lifetime.

Thank you Oskar, for being someone I can always count on, even though we were both fooled by Grace and I was hurt a lot. I'll bet you have your fair share of pain to cope with post-Grace, especially now all this shit has come to light from the newly opened windows of my memory.

I confided in Eleanor next. The fact that I liked women was obvious to Eleanor as well!

Eleanor said with not an ounce of judgment, "Well, I could've told you you like women!"

I thought it funny that my romantic preference came as no surprise, apparently to anyone. I had crossed a line with a practitioner, so I knew I would have to speak with Cotton. I was grateful when Eleanor offered to speak with Cotton for me first. Yet another night meeting was upon us, and Cotton called me into a private room with a translator. Eleanor gave me a wink for good luck as I left the main room. I knew Cotton was not going to be happy. I have to say though, by the time she spoke with me, I no longer felt ashamed about having been in a relationship with a woman. I was actually feeling proud, happy, and excited because I had found out something new about myself, something that felt "just right" in the way of *Goldilocks and the Three Bears*. Yes, in retrospect, I should have known since I was a little kid that I am not straight. I never considered it a possibility. I frequently wondered why I had awkward feelings with girlfriends. I thought it was social anxiety—I was simply socially awkward. Nope. Gay. I had crushes. Makes perfect sense to me now. I often condemned myself for feeling weird with friends and in other social situations. Why couldn't I just relax? My anxiety in part stemmed from ignorance of my sexual orientation —the feelings traditionally felt towards the opposite sex, I was getting relative to the same sex. But I did not identify the feelings as romantic or sexual, I just felt very uncomfortable.

I went into the private room where Cotton was with the translator. Eleanor had given me the wink. I kneeled. The room was much like other private rooms at bookshops, same yellow vinyl flooring, a darker golden mat on the floor, ruddy clay on the walls for good vibes, and a heated floor. Cotton looked at me seriously. I likely could not hold back my sheepish grin. I was excited about the fireworks I had felt in the kiss with Aphrodite and what the fireworks might mean for me.

Cotton asked, "Vada, why did you try to have a relationship with a practitioner?"

I apologized for that part. Cotton was biting her tongue and could barely sit still because she was so riled up.

"But it was a *woman*!" she blurted out before correcting herself. "It was a *practitioner*!"

I responded excitedly, "I know, right!?"

I was just as flabbergasted. I could see Cotton was uncomfortable with the idea that I had romantic feelings for women. Cotton had very bad pain in her body, poor digestion, and headaches from stress. I was the one who had been administering care for her. Trained in holistic wellness practices based in eastern medicine, I had used the techniques to treat Cotton's symptoms which necessitated touching Cotton's body. Cotton was too uncomfortable with this new information regarding my sexual preference and suggested I move to a new region where there were more English-speakers. I thought it was a great idea. I wanted the fuck out of there! I was ready to move on.

Off to yet another state I moved in May 2012, marking my ninth and final year of service at Beescrit Books. This time, I landed in Philadelphia. As usual, in under an hour, I moved my stuff all out, and packed it all in. Before I knew it, I was somewhere entirely new. New people, new residence, new bookshops, new everything, but I had really loved the Bronx and the people there. *Big shout to all you badass angels!*

In the new region of Beescrit Books, all instructors spoke English fluently and were under forty years old. I picked up Mark, the Regional Director, from the bookshop he was working at in a beautiful, historical, and artistic part of the bustling city. Mark greeted me warmly. We took our time getting back to the house and Mark showed me around the new dwelling. The house felt more lived-in than any of the others. Mark brought me to my room. Hard to believe, it had TWO closets, a full mattress, plenty of space, and a window opening out to a roof which Mark encouraged me to climb onto if I felt like it. I looked at Mark, silent.

"Culture shock, I know," Mark said.

I had been sleeping on the floor for at least four or five years. Mark was clean, well-spoken, bright, good-humored, sincere and kind. He was also handsome, tall, and had good muscle tone. The young male instructors in the region did something they plainly called *"jumping"*—a word they coined as their own private Beescritspeak. The young men found objects in the street to try hopping on top of or over. It was both funny and impressive to watch them. I tried once, but I fell on my ass and determined the risk of injury was not worth it to me.

Mark eased me into work in the region and did not pressure me about making money. We all knew we had to achieve our financial goals if we wanted to continue living with the bit of freedom, openness, and comfort Mark's management style established. I did okay at the bookshop that I managed as Lead Instructor, not great, but good enough.

Mark encouraged use of computers with shared Google documents and spreadsheets for business meetings. Sometimes we took a shot of sake. Sometimes we watched a movie - in ENGLISH - together! Sometimes we cooked out, or sat around a fire in the yard. Sometimes we went out dancing. We even had a Christmas tree. More of our night meetings were held at restaurants where the bookshop picked up the tab. The hierarchy was still respected, but Mark created an environment where individuality and personal freedoms were permitted, unlike other regions. *How nice it was!*

CHAPTER 28

The Gays

Not convinced of my gayness, I entered a relationship with a young instructor in the region named Philip. It did not last long. If not 100% gay, I prefer to date women. I felt badly for the young man. He had high hopes that our romance would make relationships within Beescrit more commonplace by positive example, but I was more curious about the fireworks in the kiss with Aphrodite. I had moved in with Mark and the other instructors in the spring, begun a relationship, broke it off, and found myself traipsing the gay scene by summer.

August 2012: Mark was away for the weekend at a meeting for Regional Directors. Having other English-speakers immediately around our homey home and Mark's desire to make Beescrit more congenial for more people created an emotional space for our colleagues which gave me an outlet to spend time with others identifying outside of heterosexual norms.

I was in the dark at the outset of my excursion into the curvy realm of varying gender identities and sexual preferences. Before I went out on the town with the gays, I phoned a distant friend, the only gay person I knew who might be willing to speak with me out of the blue after years of radio silence. We had worked together at the coffee shop way back when I was a teenager. I told her of my prospective gayness and she gave me great advice.

"It is about the person," she explained. "It is not necessary to think of things as gay or straight. It is about who you connect with and who you love; just look for that."

Some solid advice.

I found a gay-leaning club on the internet. I arrived too early and no one was there. I grabbed a bite at the club's restaurant. Well, at least I had tried! It was a win already. I ordered a glass of wine with my dinner and asked the mildly flamboyant waiter about how the gay scene operated.

He pointed to black painted double doors, "At ten o'clock, the doors will open and the party will start for the night."

The waiter suggested I get a hand stamp at the door before I left, so I could return later and dodge the club's cover charge. The waiter asked what kind of girls I liked. Ambiguous about the question, I said I guessed I liked girls that were like girls. The waiter assured me there were plenty of those types around and encouraged me to come back after ten.

I finished my dinner, got my hand stamped and hit the city streets. I had an hour and a half to kill and was trying to stay calm even though I was excited. Navigating the city wasn't hard. To me, now accustomed to New York City, this city was small. A cigar and wine bar caught my attention. Loosened up after having already stretched the tightness of acceptable behavior of an instructor at Beescrit Books, I decided I'd hang at the cigar bar and further contemplate if I were ready to experience the gays. A sweet mini-cigar and two glasses of wine later, I was ready for the gays. I figured that I'd just dance and enjoy myself. After all, there was no pressure to meet anyone on my first try.

A girl named Luna came to talk with me at the club. She asked if I wanted a drink and I requested water. Luna went to get me a bottle. In the meantime, another girl came to talk and tried to dance with me. I didn't feel good about the second girl so I told her I was with someone as soon as I saw Luna walking back towards me from the bar. I danced with Luna all night. We shared surface stories from our lives by shouting closely in each other's ears because the music was loud. Luna and I agreed to meet again for dinner at this same place. *My first gay date!*

I asked to speak with Mark privately when he returned from the Regional Directors meeting. Mark would have to be on board if I started dating. Mark and I sat comfortably on the built-in, wrap-around bench of the raised deck at the Beescrit residence, facing the house on a bright summer day in August. Mark greeted me warmly and spoke in his light-hearted manner of various wonders with a dose of magic-in-moderation so typical of him.

Mark is stunning, shining like a magnificent and benevolent dark star. Dark in a cozy way relative to his warmth. Big, not only in stature but in presence. I think Mark knew it and was not sure what to do with the power of his being; he could see how he affected people. He wasn't arrogant—I'd call him a kind joyful force. I told Mark it felt important for me to explore a same-sex relationship and that I'd just met someone but would not proceed unless I had his support. Though Mark's joy and charm remained in the forefront, his body shifted, and I knew Mark was internally torn. Mark's opening response was in accordance with the hierarchy and standards for living within Beescrit.

Mark said, obviously trying hard not to break my spirit, "Vada, it would be like me suddenly deciding I wanted to be a father, and I needed to have the experience."

Mark's response informed me that my "coming out" was somewhat difficult for him to conceive.

Then Mark unexpectedly added, "But you should never let anyone tell you what to do, especially if something feels important to you."

I thanked Mark, and we shot bows and arrows together at the target in the yard. *He missed his mark, but I struck the bull's eye.*

I started exclusively dating Luna soon after my conversation with Mark. The young instructors in the region were excited for me, joking with me like brothers when I went out with Luna, reminding me to "use protection." I had no intention of bringing Luna to Beescrit Books or connecting Luna with Beescrit in any capacity. Luna was curious about my friends though, so I invited one of the young male instructors, George, to join us for lunch on a weekend; he would be good company. George ended up talking about the bookshop and encouraged Luna to attend a Beescrit class. He asked why I had not already insisted Luna do so because it is so wonderful. Luna agreed and was very interested in attending a class. *Super. Thanks George.* George was very good company though, for real. I tried to see George once not long after I had left Beescrit, but found myself too angry; my dear friend seemed more entangled in Beescrit than when I had last seen him. George is such a fine man! It is heartbreaking for me to remember the good people still trapped in Beescrit Books. They think they are sacrificing themselves for humanity but the truth is that they are being abused.

I was sent off the grid on retreat to a newly acquired Beescrit property while working under Mark and dating Luna. We gave the staff at the retreat our cellphones. Gathered at the off-grid-spot were instructors who had become *stagnant* with many years spent within the confines of Beescrit Books For Wellness or those vulnerable to exiting Beescrit. I determined this myself, of course; Beescrit did not say it. The retreat opened with the CEO giving each person in attendance an opportunity to speak. I told everyone about Babo when it was my turn. *Fuck it. All's quiet on the western front.*

I may have been famous for posing challenging questions to those in authority at these types of Beescrit retreat gatherings. These questions flustered high-level instructors and often got me scolded, but I wanted to know the fucking answers. I was devoted, 100% devoted to this shit. *"Beginner's mind—no matter how many years you're in, you gotta keep an open mind and assume nothing, right?"*

I had asked Beescrit's CEO during a lecture once, "What if the True Teacher dies, what happens then?"

The translator communicated my question to the CEO who dropped the ball with his facial expression alone, dumbfounded. I received a phone call from the CEO's translator after the lecture with a response, not an answer, to my question. The translator explained that the CEO was concerned about me; the CEO thought maybe I wasn't *stable.* I reassured her and him that I was fine; I just wanted to know the answer to the question for myself.

The CEO conveyed a message through the translator: "The True Teacher is the True Teacher. And if anything ever happens to him, The True Teacher has granted spiritual law to a woman in Korea who will assume his role."

"Great, thanks."

I pretended to buy it. What else was I supposed to do? I promised myself I would never leave Beescrit Books. *I would die doing work for humanity and the Earth.*

Anyway, Luna waltzed into the bookshop one day. *Gasp!* Of course, she loved it. It is lovely and the people who gather at the bookshop are commonly lovely. It was hard managing both, Beescrit and my relationship with Luna, but it worked out because Luna participated in many Beescrit activities. Luna and I dated for a full year, then she wanted to visit her family and bring me along to meet them. Luna's family lived in another country. Personal vacations were unheard of in Beescrit, but I brought the idea to Mark and he agreed to let me do it. Mark was in rare form at the time. He disappeared randomly for almost a month and told us to take care of everything. This worked out for me though and I booked the trip.

GIRLFRIEND / LUNA

CHAPTER 29

Take A Break

In a foreign city with Luna for her nephew's graduation from college, I got a phone call from my soon-to-be roommate, Tabitha. Any other time during the trip I would not have had access to a computer or phone service. Tabitha informed me the CEO was flying out to visit our region. We both knew without saying that my absence was a problem. *Hmmm. What a conundrum!* Mark called next. He sent me paperwork for a request for a vacation—the one I was already taking. I knew he had to try to cross his Ts as best he could because my absence spelled trouble for him too.

When I returned to the United States, Mark let me settle in for a short time, before calling me to his room. We shot the shit and prepared to smoke some marijuana. It had been a long time since I had smoked the ganja. There was no need to discuss the CEO's visit and me being in another country.

Mark just said, "Vada, they want you to move back to work with Cotton."

Breathing out a raspberry laugh with my response, I voiced, "No way. Absolutely not happening."

Mark looked at me with huge warm and compassionate eyes, his own repercussions of the situation clearly present. Mark's gaze reflected what I knew to be true: it had been already decided.

I thought about going back to work under Cotton. By now, I had dedicated my life and put loads of energy into my work at Beescrit for nearly a decade. I liked helping people and being part of Beescrit's *"vision for a healthier, happier, more peaceful world."* I had come this far and had promised myself I would never quit. I called Luna to let her know my predicament and that I would likely be moving away. Luna was sad but said she would support my decision. Luna suggested I think about what I really wanted and whatever it was she would accept it.

Working again with Cotton was definitely not my first choice, but I wasn't done with Beescrit either. Mark was ordered to wrap things up with practitioners in the region. A new position awaited him, requiring travel across the nation doing workshops at Beescrit bookshop locations and other venues belonging to or rented by Beescrit Books. Blue, a new Korean Regional Director appeared. I told Blue my decision. I did not want to go back to work with Cotton; I wanted to stay in the region and continue the work I was doing *"helping people live more happy, healthy, and peaceful lives through the highly effective Beescrit practices for wellness."* Blue presented rules for working under her. Rules relative to business I accepted without question; however, rules pertaining to my personal life were a no-go. I would not agree. Blue did not know what to do with me. I was not quitting, but I gently refused to be complicit with this intrusion upon my personal life. I was firm but nice enough.

The Beescrit CEO flew across the country to meet with me personally. It was a woman named Caitlin. I picked Caitlin up from the airport, a forty minute drive from the rural bookshop I was tending to. We traveled back to the shop together. When we arrived, Caitlin wanted to do sincerity training. I obliged, arranging a short octagonal veneered wooden table with a bowl of water and incense in a room featuring symmetrically slanted ceilings. Facing the short table, I placed two half-inch foam mats in mint green cotton cases on the shiny hardwood floor, Caitlin's mat ahead of mine in accordance with requisite etiquette. Caitlin and I mechanically bowed down towards the floor, then went down onto our knees from standing, flattening ourselves like pancakes with our knees tucked under our bodies. We did this one hundred and three times. A one-hundred-three sincerity prostration practice was common, as were eighty-one, twenty-one, nine, and three times. One thousand or three thousand times in one session was less commonplace. Beescrit gee-doe-jahs do sincerity practice at least once a day, usually in the morning, *"offering their mind for what they will create for Beescrit Books' virtuous goal in regard to money and people."* This offering of the mind is called *shimgo*.

I happily completed one hundred and three sincerity prostrations with Caitlin. When we were done, she turned around and faced me. Both of us sat cross-legged on our mint green mats.

"Why are you and Blue having trouble coming to an agreement?" Caitlin asked me.

"I am willing to follow Blue's rules for business management," I said, "but not the rules seeking to control my personal life choices." I continued passionately, "Caitlin, I really want to do this work helping others, working for the beautiful goal of Beescrit Books, but I just cannot be controlled that way, not anymore."

Caitlin replied, "I know how you lived before you joined Beescrit Books and I am afraid you would die if you'd leave us."

Politely harboring a giggle, I told Caitlin, CEO, "I appreciate and understand your concern, and I most certainly will die whether I leave Beescrit Books or not."

I could tell Caitlin was having a hard time buying her own fresh-out-of-the-oven, steaming hot bullshit prior to my response.

I repeated to Caitlin that I did not want to leave Beescrit, but also clarified that I would not allow my personal life to be controlled by Blue.

Caitlin quickly wrapped it up saying, "Okay great, so you will work it out with Blue then."

I nodded.

I then drove Caitlin back to the airport, dropped her off, drove back to the rural bookshop, and received a video call from Blue. Blue gave me the exact same rules, and I gave Blue the exact same answers I had before. It appeared I had thrown a wrench into the gears of Blue's brain. Her head actually twitched a little, poor thing. I was perfectly pleasant and willing; I just would not allow my personal life to be controlled any longer, not to the same extreme as it had been so far. Blue excused herself from our video call and within about a minute Caitlin was calling me:

"Can you come back to the airport, Vada-nim?"

What the fuck did I care.

"Sure thing," I said.

On my second trip to the airport that day I enjoyed the ridiculousness of events unfolding and wondered what Caitlin was going to say. Caitlin came out from the terminal, got in my hatchback, and we found a parking lot. Once parked, I turned towards Caitlin.

She began, "Vada, you said you were going to work it out with Blue." Caitlin was slightly annoyed and seemed confused.

I explained, "I was willing to work it out, but Blue was unwilling to negotiate."

"Maybe you need to take a break, three months," Caitlin finally said.

Caitlin wished me the best as I dropped her back off at the terminal.

A break. Yeah, no. This was it. My time in Beescrit Books For Wellness had all but come to an end in the parking lot of an airport. Smoking cigarettes in alleyways and abandoned havens in Manhattan, I had already breathed a few sighs of nostalgic freedom. And in the Bronx, a vibrato of environmental factors conducted by the hurricane and the Philharmonic Orchestra inspired Autonomy and I to sing a few notes a cappella. Mark's management style was a parade of deliverance and with the security of Luna's support and respect along my route of procession, I courageously blew my novice bagpipe in the parking lot of the airport with Caitlin. I suppose I had been prepared for this moment though I had no cognizance of it at the time. I was sad my time was ending at Beescrit because I knew I would miss helping people. Luna was happy, though, and her support softened the blow of this loss.

Nature always calms my nerves, so I regularly visited a reservation nearby the rural bookshop. On a recent visit there, I climbed to the highpoint overlooking the city to photograph it. A woman arrived at the top of the hill just after me. She sat in the snow, eyeing the always magnificent view.

RESERVATION

CHAPTER 30

The Underground Railroad

Once again, I had no fucking clue what I was going to do. I sat in the garden at Luna's apartment and called Felix, an acquaintance who had recently *exited* Beescrit. Felix suggested I bargain for a severance. A severance would not only help me get back on my feet, but it might also ameliorate any bitterness I'd undoubtedly harbor towards Beescrit. I'd be able to think, *Well, at least I got that from those sons of bitches.* Seemed reasonable. I had grievances for sure but was grateful for what I had received from Beescrit and did not want to feel angry about my experiences later. Beescrit gave me disciplined and defined purpose, so, despite the brainwashing, I felt in some ways in its debt. I didn't want my Beescrit experience to haunt me. I called Oskar and told him I needed help, vaguely describing the situation. At the time, I did not think Beescrit Books was a cult. Nope. That would take me years to accept. On the heels of Felix's advice came Oskar's. My father wisely advised me to acquire an employment attorney.

I told Susan B. Glennon, attorney at law, what I could about my situation. I imagine I was emotionally guarded. Susan actively and mostly silently scoured books and the internet in front of me. Distinctly appalled by what I shared with her, Susan searched statutes of limitations on certain matters. Susan advised me to compile a list of grievances which felt complete and put a dollar value next to each one. Whatever I thought was a good amount for my grievances involving Babo, double that number. It would have been a hell of a case, but from a legal standpoint, too much time had passed. Statute of limitations. I did not know at that time, but I had mixed up the years and my case could have been pursued legally. Susan said she was willing to speak with Beescrit's human resource department on my behalf, but encouraged me to do it myself, to put my foot down in a sense. I am very glad I called HR myself. The call to Beescrit's human resource department solidified my choice to leave Beescrit and quelled my fear *"of losing the fast track to spiritual growth the True Teacher provided through Beescrit bookshop operations."* I was afraid *"I would not grow anymore without Beescrit Books or I would grow slowly as a human being."*

Oh, and by the way, this is a complete lie, Beescrit gee-doe-jahs. I found the opposite to be true. I have grown far more outside Beescrit than I had when I was isolated and squashed inside it.

I called HR and listed my grievances. Beescrit Books For Wellness expressed their apathy towards my wellbeing by replying:

"We already knew about those things. And that is why we removed Babo from Beescrit. What do you want?" the HR representative asked me next, maybe even in the same breath.

This is HR at Beescrit Books For Wellness, my one and only call. My grievances included sexual manipulation, coercion, sleep deprivation, and various other forms of abuse, all of which the company admittedly already knew about.

Are you fucking kidding me? Thanks for offering your support after I was raped for years by my superior in your organization, rape grafted with your organization's spiritual principles. What the actual fuck? What's that about humanity and the Earth? Fuck you! How long did you wait for my call? I will tell you how long, six years, maybe longer. All the while you looked me in the eye, hugged me, told me I was beautiful, and pretended you did not know. It wasn't just Itchee—at least he never hugged me—it was many. Cotton let me suffer alone. I was so stupid to think that she loved me when she was a mere tourniquet to my being bled out through exhausted exploitation.

HR begrudgingly gave me severance pay… but still, my heart rate dropped to zero.

It took me thirty minutes to realize Beescrit had already known my grievances, all of them! Before I spoke about Babo at the recent retreat I had attended for the stagnant instructors, they had known, and the rest of the abuse was commonplace in the organization. *Damn! That shit still hurts. I gave you my life. I considered you my family, Beescrit.* I was playing Candy Crush in a papasan chair in an attic of the bookshop, enjoying the idea that I was almost done at Beescrit, knowing I needed not push myself further, when it hit me. I rushed into the bathroom and let out a single cry like an elongated moose call. My gut wrenched inward, my arms outstretched to the side and upward, then I dropped to the floor in front of the porcelain goddess. My body sobbed, ironically, I would say *with 100% energy.* The irony is that I never ever felt I had given 100% energy, no matter how many hundreds or thousands of times I tried in Beescrit exercises. On the floor in front of the toilet, sounds came out of me beyond my control. My body convulsed with rigid fluidity, my back arched back and forth while on my hands and knees. When the sounds came out I saw darkness exiting my body, looking like a formless and harmless dementor from the *Harry Potter* novels. With the darkness gone, there was room for the light to enter. There was finally a light at the end of this tunnel. I had retched out the strictures and ruthlessness of Beescrit Books, allowing a space in my soul for freedom and independence to gradually find their way in.

Alice HCI was at the bookshop with me almost every day. Alice heard me from upstairs in the attic. I don't know why these people are considered half-commitment. They basically fund Beescrit Books in one way or another. I think Alice thought I had lost my mind. Alice HCI had figured out that Luna and I were in a relationship. I may have been less credible with Alice because I hid my relationship when Luna began attending regular Beescrit classes at our location. Alice met Luna only as a practitioner, not as my girlfriend. I was very open with Alice, except about my relationship with Luna. No matter. After Alice heard my weird moose impression in the attic bathroom, she came upstairs to find me back in the papasan chair. Thinking I might never speak of any grievances after that day, I told Alice many things. I did not get the sense that she believed me. *That is okay. Alice, you were very good to me, and I am thankful for you.*

Mark's Irish exit from the area overlapped with my bow-out. It was hard on practitioners when instructors swapped roles and new instructors came to teach them the Beescrit ways to wellness. Blue took over as Regional Director in the area, but Mark had to linger because the HCIs and core practitioners would be alarmed if he'd left too quickly. Mark had an unusual and special way of connecting with practitioners and instructors, making them feel deeply loved. He continued work with Beescrit Books, traveling the nation being awesome and drawing in a bunch of people because they felt great in Mark's presence.

I found a room to rent near Luna's apartment and moved out of the rented Beescrit house without saying anything to anyone, even though I had to finish up my duties at the bookshop for a few days more. My roommate Tabitha was surprised to find my stuff gone, but she understood. One of the best decisions I have ever made was to get the hell out of there. Tabitha got out too, about a year after me.

For eighteen months I paid rent in the new region, then packed up and moved out by October 2013. I rushed this move, but not too much because the stairs were dangerously steep and narrow. The centuries-old house carried a poignant history: It had been used as slave quarters for the farm house down the street. *Huh. An appropriate place for me to have lived just then! But I was about to hitch a ride on the the Underground Railroad. A perilous journey. And who says history doesn't repeat itself?*

LAST COMMUNAL HOUSE

CHAPTER 31

Hops

Once *exited* from Beescrit Books, I found myself thinking, *What just happened and how? You choose Beescrit, and then Beescrit absorbs you into itself. Beescrit parallels addiction. With addiction you get something at first, like relaxation or less inhibitions, enabling a user to be more social, among a myriad of other potential gains. Beescrit and addiction both give participants something they need or want at the beginning. Then they steal your relationships, freedom, health, and your life. Beescrit practices for wellness undoubtedly provide benefits in the beginning, but then you become their slave. Beescrit lets you believe you chose and choose the life you live inside it. The same delusion is a symptom of alcoholism. In alcoholism you think you are choosing to drink when you aren't, every month and every day. "Vision-dahlsung! Vision-dahlsung!"*

Freed from Beescrit. Now I have to live, right? No more Beescrit financial and human resource agendas! For months after leaving Beescrit Books I was elated in the moments I remembered that I didn't need to fret about goals. I had Luna, but I did not have many friends and was mostly estranged from my family. I searched frantically within myself for something familiar of which to grab hold. Everything was different. I tried to get back into wood-burning art projects, but the store no longer sold the same wooden furniture I liked to burn. I went to buy my favorite pants only to find the store had reduced the quality of its clothing. My pants did not exist anymore. I felt like I had come out of a time capsule. The only thing that hadn't changed was alcohol.

It is said alcoholism is a progressive disease. In my experience the speculated progression of alcoholism is accurate.

I got really drunk a handful of times during my years at Beescrit. When it was even possible on a short leash, I drank a couple of beers to give myself a sense of freedom and a buzz for my head. Then there were five or six bad drunken episodes—five I can remember. When I got drunk on those occasions, it was not the same as when I got drunk when I was nineteen. Alcohol affected me far worse than it had when I was younger. I picked up alcohol as a near daily habit after exiting Beescrit Books. Control of how much I drank and when I would stop frequently slipped through my fingers. Because of my alcohol consumption, the extent of the troubles I caused myself progressed and intensified.

I kept in touch with Tabitha. She told me that her first mentor at Beescrit Books, Liam, was coincidentally opening a bookshop—not a Beescrit one—in the same town where I was living. Liam had *exited* Beescrit Books For Wellness years before, but our paths crossed and we were re-acquainted. I put the address in my GPS, his bookshop just a two minute drive from my place. I figured I would stop over. Luna came with me. There was a sign on the door of Liam's bookshop: BACK IN 10 MINUTES. I decided to wait and he appeared. He was happy to see me and greeted me by name. I was a bit surprised that Liam had remembered me because we had been on two very different paths in Beescrit. Liam had a big personality and was fast-tracked as a leader; whereas, I had gone the other way, trying to be as small as possible but still contribute to Beescrit's goal.

Liam suggested I try a daily class. His bookshop was absent of sales consultation pressures and practitioners wore what they wanted. Liam bolstered his bookshop offerings with colorful self-help methods and barely spoke of Beescrit Books but would talk about it with me when I wanted to. I attended a class at the bookshop. Afterwards, Liam described me as a Mercedes Benz and offered me a job teaching at his bookshop. I would have to start working, so I decided to ease myself in and took on teaching two classes a week.

After teaching for two weeks, Liam told me he wanted to take a full-time job requiring travel and asked if I would be willing to care for the bookshop full-time. I knew what this meant, and Liam knew that he was guaranteed a good worker in me. It was the holiday season and I would take over the bookshop in the New Year.

CHAPTER 32

Say Grace

Luna hopelessly wanted me to have closeness with Grace. I explained Grace and I were doing just fine, above average even. I agreed to have Luna come with me for Christmas dinner at Grace's house. Luna was looking forward to it. Since she would be there I thought the risk of anything weird happening was reduced, that the visit with Grace would be fine. I was doing well: I had *exited* Beescrit Books For Wellness, procured a new job, had my own place now, and was in a relationship. Unfortunately, things weren't so fine at Grace's. We exchanged gifts. I asked about my brother Owen, how he was doing. Grace shot her mouth off something quick involving Oskar relative to Owen. Oskar, to whom Grace had not spoken in nine years. I suggested we keep the conversation about Owen alone.

Grace stood, already reeling, "You are always defending him [Oskar]!" she said on the cusp of crazed, shaking from her anger.

I stood and said, "Come on, Mom, I'm sorry."

Things got quickly out of hand. It was my refusal to react to anything Grace said about Oskar. Grace was losing it because I would not engage with her. I was surprised this was happening because Luna was there, but Luna quickly faded into the background as the necessity of my addressing my mother's frustration became paramount. Grace said many not-very-nice things to me in her fury. There were plenty of profanities directed at me.

"Get out of my house," Grace said. "I never want to see you ever again!"

Grace went upstairs to her bedroom. Standing in the living room with Luna, I called to my mother, begging her to please come back down and not let this be the last time we would see each other. Grace refused vocally from her bedroom, and I sent my fist through Grace's brand new drywall at the bottom of the stairs. I am twenty-nine years old at this time.

After more begging on my part, Grace made her way downstairs descending at a normal pace, but once she stepped onto the living room floor, she came at me. I spotted Grace's windup and karate-chop-blocked her attempted strike.

We froze for one second, "Did you just try to hit me?"

With what I can only describe as hatred in her eyes, body language, and tone; Grace said with a straight face, "You deserve it."

Grace stepped back, her back to the fireplace, throwing a tantrum and wallowing in self-pity. Finally she moaned, "No one understands me."

I offered my most compassionate understanding of Grace from what I had gathered up to this point. I told Grace I thought she had always had a hard time with her depression. My Uncle Colton's death, her only sibling, dampened her ability to be the mother she wanted to be. I reassured Grace we both wanted the same things, to love and be loved. First, Grace denied what I said, but then it flipped over in her mind. I could see the shift by a slight change in her expression.

"Yes, that is it," Grace said eerily calmly before returning to a rant riddled with self-pity.

I explained to Grace that her life was right now. I asked Grace when she would start living, putting the past behind her, and begin finding happiness. Grace continued to alternate between anger and self-pity even after concurring with the empathetic story I'd presented. Grace continued calling me bad names and insisted before going back upstairs that she never wanted to see me again.

It was intense. I felt like an animal needing to shake itself off after a fight. I texted a friend who worked in construction to see how much it'd cost to fix a spot of drywall about the size of my fist and left Grace $50.00 to fix the hole I'd made. No stranger herself to traumatic events, Luna was nevertheless shaken by my interaction with Grace—quite telling of the intensity of the situation.

Still shaken, Luna commented, "You did a good job with your mom. I cannot believe how positive you stayed with her."

My mind was far away from myself so the comment came as a surprise. Instead, I was wrapt in concern for Grace, aware I needed to do something to shake it off and get myself back on track because Luna was there. I drove to a mountain reservation parking lot. The car was barely in park, I opened my car door as wide as it would go, blasted some song loudly, and ran without hesitation into a field of grass. I moved my body to the music in the field, unaware of anything other than bringing myself back to myself in a rush for Luna's sake.

After that Christmas hullabaloo, Luna ceased suggesting overtures of my reuniting with my mother. Grace called the next day and apologized, perhaps for the first time ever. I think it was because Luna had witnessed the episode. Apologies are not a thing Grace does. Grace taught me that "sorry doesn't make it," meaning an apology does not make anything better. Eleanor is the one who taught me how to say, "I am sorry," in a meaningful way when I was twenty-six years old.

I thought about what had transpired at Grace's house. Logically I would never recommend anyone to involve themselves with a person who treated them the way Grace treated me, even if the person happens to be her parent, so I thought I should take my own advice. Besides, Grace could not control herself in front of me, and I believed Grace had not intended to behave as she had. To save my mother the guilt, and myself the trouble, I physically removed myself from my mother's life. I instead sent text messages on requisite days like Mother's Day, holidays, and her birthday; so she couldn't off herself and blame it on me.

What a perfect time to dive into a new career in business management in the arena of self-help! Liam knew not to pressure me about making money or doing consultations at his bookshop. He was increasingly absent from the bookshop as his new career took much of his time. When Liam was in town, we brainstormed. I wrote down Liam's good ideas and then off I went implementing them. It was way more fun to manage Liam's bookshop than Beescrit Books. At his bookshop I had freedom and was paid fair wages. Bereft of unreasonable financial goals, I was able to continue helping people feel better within themselves with various self-help methods. Some wellness techniques practiced at Liam's bookshop were similar to those offered at Beescrit Books, but the bulk of the methods were different. I did not have to learn all the techniques; I just needed to find people good at teaching the techniques and hire them. Wellness having become a fad by this time, persons to hire were readily available.

I drank most evenings after work for a couple of hours until I passed out. As my alcoholism progressed, I passed out less and stayed awake more. This was unnerving because I would wake up in terror, memories of the night before trickling back into my awareness. Usually though, nothing bad happened and I was a jovial type of drunk.

Luna was sad at first. She did not understand why I suddenly plunged into the bottle, smoked cigarettes, and occasionally smoked marijuana in tandem. She thought I was turning into a different person. The social norms of her country informed Luna that people who smoke marijuana are drug addicts. I could not understand why she did not understand why I wanted to drink. Drinking felt like the only way to take back the semblance of myself. She and I moved in together, but things were not going smoothly. She took a trip for a few weeks to visit her family. Upon her return, she wanted to try smoking marijuana.

Luna toked a bit and said, "I just feel relaxed."

I said, "Precisely, that is it."

I think she was pleasantly surprised by the non-lightning-thunderbolt experience of marijuana.

Luna and I split up and things went downhill in my alcoholism, then up again, then way, way down. I dated four or five girls for short periods of time, was promiscuous with select men, and then I met Sofia. Sofia lived seven-hours away by plane with no direct flights, in another country. Sofia and I met at a bar when she was visiting a friend in the United States. When I met Sofia, Liam was coincidentally encouraging me to take a vacation. I decided to ask Sofia how she felt about me visiting her. Sofia was happy and so I went. We had a nice visit, and decided to try a long distance relationship which proved exhausting and expensive, leaving me with credit card debt. Sofia was high-maintenance, to say the least. There is a meme about women from her country that summarizes Sofia succinctly:

The sweetest, most beautiful, loving, amazing, evil, psychotic creature you'll ever meet.

Non-long-distance was the ideal. I met with immigration attorneys and public counselors regarding how to legally get Sofia into the country to see if we could coexist for real, a feat which never came to fruition. Sofia and I were engaged after one year of dating and by our second anniversary we had planned an engagement party even though we still lived apart. Sofia was coming to the United States to meet my friends. By now, I had made some really good ones, friends who would save my life, including my ex-girlfriend Luna.

Hallelujah and Amen!

SOFIA

CHAPTER 33

G'head

BLOODY MARY

early enough

After I had worked three years with Liam, he wanted to sell the bookshop, but he didn't say that. Instead he messed with bookshop procedures while secretly preparing to sell. He altered my role, leaving staff and practitioners without answers. It was frustrating for everyone.

The business grew two hundred fifty percent in two years and by the third year Liam wanted to sell. I wanted to buy the bookshop from him. I became passionate about a new self-help modality and wanted to proceed with developing my new skill. A friend from the bookshop, Cora, would be my business partner. After negotiations, Liam agreed to sell to us, before backing out of the deal ten days before we closed it. Cora and I did not feel great about the situation, but we both agreed to stay on in our roles at Liam's bookshop. I called Oskar to vent about the process. Oskar advised me, as Oskar does when I ask for help. I probably would have been okay had I not ended up drunk and pissed off before next phoning Liam. Our conversation did not go well. I spoke impolitely, loudly, and with vulgarity. I felt hurt that he no longer cared about what we had built together. Liam expressed much gratitude over the years for my work and called me his golden goose. I felt saddened that he had lost his respect and gratitude for me. I was sad. In a drunken stupor, I lit our relationship on fire and watched it burn. Afterwards, Cora and I would make moves for opening our own bookshop.

Exactly one month after my drunken conversation with Liam, I sat in meditation in the morning. I meditated at least once a day, often asking myself if I was safe to continue drinking or not. I never got a clear answer, until this unusually mild winter day in December 2016. When in the confines of my cozy room above my friend Stella's garage in suburbia, I heard a voice from within, "Go ahead and drink exactly the way you want to, Vada, and see what happens." *Yip! Sounds good to me.*

No matter how many stupid and scary things happened because of my drinking, I was always able to convince myself it was fine for me to drink again. What's one or two beers? The problem was, I'd become a full-fledged alky. When? Not sure, but there I was with the blessing from within to go ahead, to drink with complete abandon. I can't recall the time that I started drinking that day, but it began with Bloody Marys. *Early enough.*

I was at home where I lived above the garage, an apartment I was renting for three months. After two or three vodkas, I reached into the backseat of my car, deciding to finish off the two cans of beer leftover from the night before. I could control my drunkenness if I stuck with one type of alcohol on a given day, but this day was different—no rules. After the beers, I went into the house to pour another Bloody Mary. I liked to drink in my parked car so I could smoke cigarettes and be warm. My roommate Stella, a single mother lovingly cooking a wholesome meal for her family, opened a bottle of champagne and offered me a glass. Lady that I am, I graciously obliged. We killed the bottle and Stella popped another cork. I refilled my empty glass and topped off what was left in hers from the fresh bottle. *Faux pas, Vada! Combining fresh and bubbly on top of old and flat—that is no way to treat champagne!* Correcting my mistake, I just gulped down Stella's glass and poured her a fresh one.

Finishing my champagne, I made yet another Bloody Mary and headed back to the car to smoke a cigarette while Stella put her two young children to bed. I was reeling drunk and cursing something ungodly. In a disconnected state because of the booze, I called Eleanor. We rehashed some old, nasty Beescrit stuff.

"Not everyone has those types of experiences here at Beescrit Books," Eleanor said.

I fucking love Eleanor and remember that the phone call left me helpless and sad for her. My heart lit on fire to hear so intimately and directly her rattle off Beescrit's mantras of bullshit, fouling Eleanor's amazing and beautiful self. And I know Eleanor loves me.

After hanging up with Eleanor and unsure of what to do with my feelings, I convinced someone I hardly knew to meet me at the only place open late in suburbia, a lone bar called G'head.

CHAPTER 34

Evel Knievel

The approximately three years and four months of drinking post-Beescrit were golden, overflowing with Yuengling for the most part. Every once in a while I'd go on a tequila kick, ya know, if I had a cold. *A couple shots of tequila will clear you right up!* Problem was, I'd drink the entire bottle in a few hours. In one night, if the tequila ran dry, I'd suck down whatever was still around if the bars were closed.

I clearly had the feeling that I was in control when I suddenly switched from drinking to drowning. A two beer limit would quickly turn into a six-pack. I had no intention of downing twelve or eighteen beers 'til I 'fell asleep' at night, only to wake up for a full day's work and start the vicious cycle all over again. I had held six jobs before my drinking ended—one full time and five part time. In part due to drinking, my full-time job at Liam's bookshop would also end.

There I was one month after leaving work at Liam's bookshop with my personal internal approval to drink myself to oblivion. After that phone call with Eleanor, I made just one more Bloody Mary and put it in the backseat of my car for later. I left to meet the near stranger at the G'head—a ten-minute drive from my apartment. It was after 11:00 p.m.

I did not make it to the bar. Instead, I started passing out while I was driving. The police apparently tried to pull me over, but I sped straight ahead at more than fifty miles per hour onto an active construction site, hit a three-foot pile of debris, sending my car airborne where it crashed into the back of a stationary dump truck. I was aware of the motion of my upper body all the way forward, then all the way back. When I realized my car was stopped, my automatic inclination was to get the hell out of there, but I quickly realized that this was not an option. In front of me I saw squares in a wall—the back of the dump truck, the cracked windshield, and my deployed airbags. Then I sensed the blood start pouring down my face from my eyes and nose. I wiped my nose with the sleeve of my green velvet jacket as if to put on a good face.

The police working construction detail for the night witnessed the entire debacle as it happened. By the time the police officer opened my driver's side door only a moment later, I knew the jig was up for me.

The police report said the officer opened my door, asked me if I was okay, and I just stared at him. I do remember what I was thinking: *Do I look okay to you? I am obviously not okay.* Apparently I got out of the car and recited my personal information to the police in a "slow and deliberate" manner, resisted the fire fighters when they arrived, and repeatedly asked:

"Who the fuck parked that dump truck in the middle of the road?"

I also repeatedly complained about how poorly lit the construction site was. I was afraid. I thought for sure that I was going to jail and my life was over. In the ambulance, I said I wanted to die. The EMTs suggested that I stop saying that before we got to the hospital, unless I wanted to be admitted for three days. *Thanks for the advice.* I did not actually want to die; I just did not want to face the crippling reality of my fucked up self, and I hadn't even realized the worst parts of the situation yet. *Heart rate dropping to zero!*

The police spoke with Stella when I called her from my cellphone at the hospital. Stella couldn't come to the hospital because the babysitter, me, was obviously unavailable. The police informed Stella that I would not be home, and that I was getting arrested. Stella thought I was playing a joke on her, that I'd gotten someone at the bar to get on the phone as a prank.

"It's not possible," Stella told the police officer, "Vada was here with me not more than an hour ago."

I called Oskar who did not answer but called me back almost immediately. Ashamed, I cried and told Oskar I was in big trouble.

Oskar asked me, "Can you move your fingers and toes?"

I checked and replied, "Yes."

"Everything will be okay, Vada."

POLICE OFFICER

CHAPTER 35

Ugly Woman

FACE ACCIDENT

CAR ACCIDENT

Nurses ran a blood test at the hospital. My blood-alcohol content was eight times the legal limit. Medically I should have been in a coma or respiratory arrest, but there I was talking and engaging with police officers, doctors, and nurses. The first hospital refused to treat me because their staff felt ill-equipped to handle the probable internal injuries from the severity of the accident. At the bottom of the sheet on my gurney was written "50+ MPH." I was taken by ambulance to another hospital in the city. I texted Luna because I knew I needed a lawyer, and Luna knew a great one. Luna pressed me about why I was asking and where I was. I told Luna, just so she'd stop asking, adding that I did not want her to come to the hospital. I called two more people, Cora (actually Cora's husband too) and Beatrix. Beatrix was my work-wife at Liam's bookshop. Cora and her husband did not answer. Beatrix was shaken from sleep by her dogs a few minutes after I called. She saw the missed call and texted me: ARE YOU OKAY? I texted Beatrix a picture of my ugly, blown-apart and bloody face with a: NOT REALLY, LOL. Beatrix did not think it was funny and came to the hospital in the middle of the night. It was around 2:00 a.m. when she arrived, just in time to hold my hand while the plastic surgeon sewed my face back together. I cried something awful. *My sincerest apologies to the nurses, doctors, and patients in the ER that night. I was at the bottom of my metaphorical barrel, absolutely. I thank you: police officers, firefighters, EMTs, and everyone who helped me at a time when I couldn't help myself, and regardless of how annoying, disruptive, and reckless I was.*

Beatrix spoke with Stella who told her the police said they were arresting me.

"How much did you drink?" Beatrix asked me.

"I think only three drinks! I do not know why this happened."

I know. A little understatement, a big lie. The champagne I'd forgotten about came back to me and the accident made a bit more sense. Beatrix told me the ER reeked of alcohol and it was coming from me. At my hospital bedside, Beatrix called Oskar to inform him of my pending arrest. I tried to stop her from saying anything more to him, but they spoke a few more moments very seriously. Oskar asked Beatrix if he needed to fly out. She told him there was nothing he could do if he did come and that she had me covered.

I miraculously had incurred no internal injuries. I suffered head and facial trauma including a broken nose with a nostril hanging by a thread and eye and forehead injuries from the airbag. At a time when a woman's beauty peaks, my face was ugly with dried blood, swelling, stitches, bruises, burns and lacerations—a cross between Godzilla and Frankenstein's. Far worse than when I'd slapped myself silly at Cotton's imperative.

Beatrix went home to get some rest and see her son off to school and told me she would come back in a few hours. *Beatrix, what an awful place to bear witness! Thank you for being there for me in one of the scariest moments of my life and that's saying a whole lot, here and now in my thirty-second year.*

Little did I know that Luna had shown up in the waiting room of the hospital. Beatrix crossed Luna's path on her way back in to check on me. Luna informed Beatrix that this was not a one-off incident, that I had been heading in this direction, which is why she'd come to the hospital. Luna thought I was lucky to be alive and, for sure, next time I'd be dead; the repercussions of my drinking would only worsen each time I was drunk. Meantime, I was sobering up and recovering more quickly than my caregivers had been expecting. They moved my bed into the hallway. I was in a neck brace and strapped with an embarrassing yellow bracelet that read in all black capital letters: FALL RISK. *Yeah, no kidding! And sadly enough, in many more ways than one.*

The hospital social worker serendipitously came to talk to me just before Beatrix walked in with Luna behind her, "Do you think you need some help? We have some resources."

"What do you mean?" I asked the social worker.

Slightly off her guard, but politely, the social worker said, "Uh, your blood alcohol content was quite high when you came in here."

I dismissed her, "I am just fine, thank you."

And I actually believed that on some level! As I spotted Beatrix and then Luna behind her, I started saying, "No..." because I realized that the worst possible thing was happening— someone besides Luna knew I could not control my drinking.

That is weird, right? Within a minute I went from denial to appalled. I intuitively knew Luna had told Beatrix about my drinking before either of them said anything at all to me. I had just verbally lied to the social worker and to myself that I did not need help. I was still in the bed in the hallway of the ER in a bright yellow plastic neck brace. Beatrix came near me, leaned over, and thrust her stern and unmarred face in my monster face. She spoke to me with a furious and powerful love I hadn't experienced before, her tone and volume clear and pointed so I would not miss a word: "How did you hide this from me?"

With a long pause and serious stare, Beatrix, containing her fiery tears, emphasized into my face: "You listen to me,

Vada! I am going to Mama-Bear the shit out of your ass. We are going to do every single thing we need to do to help you because I won't be able to live with myself if we don't."

That is pretty much an exact description of a verbatim delivery.

I went back home to the apartment above the garage. My friends operated like a well-oiled machine, organizing their efforts to help me amidst their own family responsibilities. My friends stayed with me in shifts twenty-four hours a day for three days. Beatrix was hellbent on me going to treatment and did everything in her power to get me into a facility, including calling my insurance company and researching programs. I was more thinking I could try drinking again once I addressed some of my emotional issues; maybe I would attend an outpatient program at best. Was inpatient really necessary? Well, the short answer was, yes, it was.

I got a letter in the mail from the dump truck driver's insurance company with a personal injury claim. Thankfully, he's fine; but I realized I had endangered a life, many lives, my own life too—and countless times. *How could I not see this before? I absolutely had not put two and two together. I am this person—I, Vada, who has actually eaten ants so their lives wouldn't be in vain if I'd accidentally stepped on one of them.*

Once I realized how reckless I had been, I felt like the ugliest woman in the world, not remotely alluding to the condition of my face. I don't think I had ever wanted to get away from myself more. *Self-help you by day, endanger you by night! Self-help me by day; endanger myself and everyone I care about by night! What the fuck? How was I ever going to change by just sitting above the garage?* I knew I probably wouldn't, so I went to treatment. Beatrix warmed the engine, I just had to press the gas. I did every single thing I had to do and could do. I dealt with doctors, insurance companies, the police, the division of motor vehicles, sobriety, treatment, a new therapist (Noah), and a lawyer (Frank).

Thank goodness I realized I would never be able to drink normally again. If I could have kept drinking without fear of killing myself or endangering other people, I probably would have never stopped and lived a half-alive life for the rest of my miserable days.

I met Christina in rehab. Christina was five months pregnant, didn't know it, had been smoking crack, was homeless and prostituting herself for drugs. I thought her scenario was worse than mine, but what a crock of shit that comparison was. She saved me from killing myself by substance abuse. Christina and I sat in the common area where there was a television in the treatment place. A woman—a school teacher—wriggled around on the floor unable to get comfortable, highly physically sensitive at the end of her detox from heroin. We all sort of engaged in conversation. I said something about my problems being relative to my emotions.

Christina released a dismissive scoff and asked me, "Can you stop drinking once you start?"

I answered, "Yes, as long as there is no more alcohol."

Christina followed, "You have a substance abuse problem, Sweetie!"

My brain felt like a casino, pinging and bells and whistles and flickering lights everywhere. It hit me like the back of a dump truck: *I was not a shit human being. I had a substance abuse problem.* I could not drink in safety, period, never. It would never be worth the risk to me. It seemed like a simple fix, and I was grateful for it. *Don't put this one particular type of liquid in your body. Don't endanger yourself or anyone else.*

I had initially downplayed my substance abuse relative to Christina's but then realized that we were in the exact same plight. I was just like her, and she, just like me. I will always love you, Christina, though I am sure I never told you. I am forever grateful for your presence in my life at that pivotal moment, for your perfect delivery of the truth, annihilating the thick denial of my substance abuse.

CHAPTER 36

Relatively Unscathed

Rehab was interesting. I couldn't get in anywhere covered by my insurance. Ironies of life, they wouldn't admit me because I was *NOT* drunk. Oskar helped me. I ended up in the perfect rehabilitation spot. It was not awful, but it was not nice, and I would not want to go back—just the perfect combination of experiences I had hoped for. Beatrix took on the task of communicating with Sofia and helped her decide not to come to the United States, nor to count on our engagement, or otherwise. Beatrix told Sofia I needed to focus on taking care of myself, which couldn't be truer. Beatrix said Sofia was preoccupied with herself and was one of the most manipulative people she had ever come across. Beatrix explained she knows this type of person well, and Sofia was a pro. Sofia was the least of my problems; regardless, I still loved her.

I decided I could not open a bookshop with Cora. I was in no condition and she graciously accepted my sincere regrets.

I called Owen and Oskar from rehab, maybe Jack too.

Since I hadn't called Grace, Oskar encouraged me to contact her saying seriously, "Vada, if it were my child, I would want to know."

I understood, agreed to get in touch with her, and left Grace a voicemail. It was more than a week before Grace 'reached out' to me and by then I was home from rehab. Grace didn't say a word about the accident or ask me how I was doing but she seemed happy I was sober. I think some part of Grace does care, but her shit is so fucked up that her caring turns out to be manipulative at best. *Interesting how my language gets foul just at the mention of her name!*

I continued doing everything I could to stay sober. I actively participated in daily alcohol recovery meetings. While heading into a recovery meeting one night, I bumped into a guy on his way out. He was checking behind him on his way down the stairs to the street like a super-sketch, so he hadn't noticed me. He stopped at the close-up sight of my brutalized face. He told me he knew a lawyer who had gotten him out of trouble. He gave me Frank's contact and I never saw the guy again, though I went back to the same spot hundreds of times for alcohol recovery meetings. *Thanks dude, whoever you are. A random happenstance can prove lucky sometimes.*

I met with the lawyer, Frank, whom I tried to convince that I was entirely guilty and should be punished to the fullest extent of the law. Frank explained that wasn't quite how the law worked. By the time we went to the clerk's office at the court three months had passed since the accident. I had never been formally arrested either. Because I'd been moved from one hospital to another, I think the police did not bother to follow me and pursue it. My face was healing, stitches out, though still quite swollen.

Sitting outside the clerk's office waiting to be called in, Frank asked me, "Vada, what are your plans? What are you going to do?"

I told Frank, "I want to be an artist and for all this mess to be over so I can maybe live the life I wanted."

Then, it was our turn.

If I had a tail, it would have been between my legs. The police officer, dressed in a crisp white-collared shirt, began reading the police report from the incident aloud. The clerk, wearing a navy blue fleece distinguished by the court's embroidered emblem, stopped the officer halfway through the report to glance at my attorney over his bifocals.

"That's enough," the clerk said, "Do you have anything to say?"

Frank said only that there was ample evidence for a case against me.

The clerk adjusted his gaze towards the police officer, "What do you think?"

The officer, named Pope—*I shit you not! Yeah! devout Catholics!*—said, "I was there the night of the event and I think we should do a continuance."

The clerk explained that my scenario was very serious and that I should thank my attorney.

I thanked them all. I did not know what had happened yet. Before we were excused, the clerk told me to come back with a spotless driving record in one year along with several other stipulations that I would have to do for my sobriety regardless.

Frank and I walked out of the room in silence as I followed behind him. Making our way down the stairs to the main lobby of the historical courthouse, I curiously observed the brown fabric and tailoring of Frank's suit as what had just unfolded in the clerk's office started processing in my mind.

"Uh, Frank," I cautiously whispered in an effort to contain the happiness of potential relief, erring on the side of caution, "Was that a miracle?"

Frank said he hadn't seen anything like it, especially with the blatant seriousness of the accident. My driver's license hadn't even been suspended. Frank recommended I go to the state's motor vehicle office right away to get my license. (The police had taken it on the night of the accident.) He also suggested I take private driving lessons with an instructor before

I got back on the road. For the record and to calm my nerves before I got behind the wheel again. *Brilliant. Thank you, Frank.*

I am abundantly grateful for the way this ordeal panned out and I was somehow given another chance. I meticulously did all I could to get myself help and luckily had access to the resources to do it. The house with my apartment above the garage was sold and I had to move. Before I went to court, I had to ask for help with rides to get to alcohol recovery meetings. (I was without a car after the accident.) Nearly every single day I went to a meeting for more than a year, sometimes twice a day. I pursued all recommendations for my sobriety, even the tough parts where I had to admit all the ugly stuff inside me with a trusted friend, and then become a trusted friend for other people in their own alcohol recovery. I was conscientious about the year granted me to prove myself, and nervous that I would fuck it up with a headlight out or something stupid like that.

I was never more happy to be white in my entire life. A mixed bag of emotions. Would it have made a difference had I been male, straight, old, or black? If details of my persona were altered in my story, I wonder how the courts would have ruled. I wondered why I had come out of this episode relatively unscathed from what could have been dire consequences.

Luna drove me to the court and then to the motor vehicle office. *Thank you, my friend, for helping me. And thank you for telling Beatrix about my drinking problem even though you knew I would not like it.*

CHAPTER 37

Two Flames

TINY APARTMENT

After getting sober in the winter, I officially broke up with Sofia in the summer. I started my own business and got by. During the summer, paid work slowed down and I made a goal to complete six paintings. I pounded out eight very different works. They were an explosion of pent-up angst, weirdness, grief, and love.

My new apartment was two hundred fifty square feet, including the kitchen and bathroom. I had no closet, but I was used to that, so no biggie. The kitchen morphed throughout the day: living room chill spot, photography studio, art studio, office space, dance floor, and certainly it was always the kitchen. It was tight, and I was running out of space, but I loved it. I couldn't make more paintings because there wasn't an inch to spare to keep them. The walls were hung. I either needed a bigger place or to rent a studio. Either way, I needed more money.

I contemplated what to do next and what I really wanted. Staying in the tiny apartment would be okay, but I would stay small. I preferred to work under one roof and not rent another space. In hopes my dreams of becoming an artist could come true, along with an opportunity to rent a place with plenty of space for a reasonable price, I decided to take the risk of expanding and failing, rather than staying small and continuing to barely make ends meet.

Single for a year and in a new place with plenty of room, I considered if I wanted a human companion. I thought long and hard about what type of person with whom I would want to be. Ultimately I thought it unfair to ask any human being to be in an intimate relationship with me when I knew I could not and did not want to deliver in the sex department with any type of regularity. Most times I do not feel sexual. My sexual escapades had been unfulfilling, to say the least, but then I met Evelyn.

Evelyn is a small town girl and is dedicated to her creative work in technology. Our relationship began only months before the COVID-19 pandemic of 2020. We had moved in together and then found ourselves in the unexpected lockdown. I knew Evelyn was out of her mind from the start and just my type of crazy. She visited my place for the first time, bursting through the front door with a duffel bag, actively talking with her hands, explaining about the driver that nearly killed her on her way over and the fact that the duffel bag was indicative of nothing. She was speaking passionately, loudly, and with enthusiasm—as she does almost all of the time.

She also has serious anxiety problems from many years of an eating disorder, a severely abusive relationship, and a sexual assault. I often cannot discern when Evelyn is being her naturally animated self or when her anxiety has gotten the best of her in a traumatized brain phase at which time she bends, contorts, and rehashes every word said between us. The winding conversations can last for hours despite my best efforts to disarm and reassure her. *I honestly don't know how she has the stamina for it. I am very resilient, but the stress of these conversations has worn me down and broken my threshold of tolerance.* In either case, trauma-brain or not, I sometimes perceive her in a frenzy and thus as a threat. She also rejects affection apart from sexual intimacy as a result of her trauma. In close proximity 24/7 in lockdown, Evelyn's affection-aversion mirrored my mother's rejection of me as a child. This is what initially cracked the door open to my deeply repressed reality. I first experienced an uptick in my recurring nightmares of begging for affection from someone close to me to a degree of intensity that necessitated my moving into a separate bedroom. People-pleaser that I am, I creatively take actions to sidestep my trauma symptoms in respect of hers, but the affection-rejection enmeshed with the frenzy has been for me like a fireworks display to a shell shocked war veteran.

No matter what we try, Evelyn and I bump against one another, and not in a particularly pleasurable way. No big deal though because I came to accept that Evelyn and I are twin flames, the good kind with the purpose of personal growth. *For those of you vying for your twin flame, do not worry if and when you will find her. The experience will find you when you are ready. It will be among the most challenging days of your life because you'll face yourself with such intensity.* Twin flames hum different notes seamlessly segueing the same tune, in contrast to melodies harmonizing or clashing—and there's no glitching as in other relationships. I have a sneaking suspicion that musicians Noga Erez and Ori Russo are this type of couple too. It's undeniable, no cakewalk either. The love is solid, but much time is spent wading around in personal shit storms and jumping in poop puddles. I'm patiently waiting for the part where our karma is cleaned up and we live in bliss, though we may need several lifetimes of this type of relationship to sort through it all. Unconvinced this is the finale, for us it has been absolutely worth it! *I wouldn't have known the truth about my life if she wasn't exactly the person she is.* Evelyn's got most of her sense of self, and I have maybe a little tucked away somewhere, revealing itself in the pages of this book.

Evelyn frequently blames herself for my plight of trauma symptoms, but I know that Grace and Beescrit Books are the responsible parties. Whether the conscious intention for cruelty is present or not matters little, since the results of cruelty are damaging no matter what. When the damage is exposed or stimulated, I perceive a forest fire where there is but a matchstick in real life. One of the biggest struggles for me is feeling that I have to fight a forest fire when I logically know it is the flame of one single match. The unfortunate consequence is that Evelyn's actions, innocent or not, can prompt me to turn against myself with inordinately major and unjust reactions.

Grace has covert narcissistic antisocial personality disorder. This is not a diagnosis, but Grace's symptoms best match this disorder. As an infant and child, I blamed myself for her cruelty; this mentality was my only option as a dependent with no one but a mother to rely on for care—if I had been the cruel one, then I was not in danger. My mother proclaimed that I was an extension of her. I tried hard to be perfect in hopes that the kind words my mother would hear about me from other people would prove to her that I was good. Anything less than perfection on my part, relative to my mother's unpredictable standards, was justification for Grace's mockery, soul murder, and the personal extinction of her daughter. If I lost control of my emotions amidst my mother's onslaught of twisted narratives or verbal and physical abuse, Grace told me I was showing my 'true colors'. Tragically, losing control of my emotions was sometimes the safest play to make it all stop. In this way my mother would be satisfied since I'd succumbed to behaving as the evil child she insisted I was. It is no wonder that I smack and criticize myself, demean myself, and wish to disappear. It is the reality Grace nurtured in me fundamentally as a child. Later, as an adult, a kind of juxtaposed reality was mirrored by the cult.

So when my brain thinks the abuse is occurring again my faulty fundamentals rapid fire for the 'safest' outcome. The fire alarms go off, my frontal lobes of logic incinerate, and my emotional amygdala hijacks the scene like a martyring firefighter. The ashy state of logic combined with the mobilization of the firefighter revoke my ability to rationally respond to perceived threats, frantically 'putting out fires'.

My trauma responses began intensifying in my relationship with Evelyn who is often the matchstick. In one incident, Evelyn told me that I didn't listen to her opinions enough. Due to the compounded stress between us, Evelyn's suggestion quickly set ablaze a forest fire within me as my inner critic beat the living hell out of me. I managed to excuse myself from the conversation with her, but in private I still told myself aloud with passion and self-hatred, "Vada, I hope you die today, you worthless piece of shit!" I had irrationally judged myself harshly for not having listened well enough to Evelyn's opinions and had taken full responsibility for this flaw. For this, I felt I couldn't do anything right and didn't deserve to live. Since I wouldn't kill myself, I resorted to afflicting punishment and exile on myself instead. I do all I can to manage my symptoms, but I often offer Evelyn an out because I understand my trauma can be atrocious. *However, I am beginning to realize that I am not the only person in this relationship who needs to be managing the symptoms of their trauma.*

Amidst the labyrinth of my traumatic responses I am now finally capable of finding my way out to the truth. Knowledge has me on the path to full recovery: I did not do this to myself, and behaviors such as extreme self-chastisement I learned elsewhere. Parts of me are broken and still need healing.

There is comfort to know too that it is not my fault, but I do need the strength in having to deal with it.

I was able to calm down and realize that anyone who experiences oppression or abuse could easily feel as worthless as I did. Compounded effects of oppression and abuse intensify feelings of fear, anger, and helplessness. I understood how a person could become capable of cruelty against her own kind. Oppression and abuse are inhumane; therefore they yield potentially inhumane responses for survival in individuals, relative to themselves and others.

I feel compassion, anger, disgust, and sadness in relation to my first authoritarian ruler and abuser, Grace. Compassion because Grace likely suffered abuse that caused her mental illness in an oppressive system that nurtured neglect from her start; anger because Grace's psychological state created major setbacks for me. I missed foundational human experiences when they should have been available because I was internally dilapidated, secretly living with a dissociative disorder. I am additionally disgusted by the despicably grotesque and twisted actions of my mother and the ways she continues to lie and deceive. I am finally deeply saddened that my mother lives in such a dark world, as I would feel for anyone suffering with mental illness.

Evelyn does have certain personality traits that whisper to my subconscious of Grace but she also cares deeply which wreaks havoc on my brain. My brain reads Evelyn as a threat and therefore instinctively reacts to protect me by putting myself down with brute force because that is most likely to appease my abuser, but Evelyn is steadfastly present and cares for me in contrast to Grace. Evelyn does not want me to shame myself or beat myself up. But because Evelyn's expressions and gesticulations are excited and passionate even when she's not caught in the winding spiral of her own trauma, my brain reads her demeanor as frenzied; it freaks me the fuck out, and I automatically respond as if the old abuse is happening again.

Evelyn is a key player in my process of relational healing as she presses all my buttons without intending to do so. This tumultuous process is proving the most challenging work of my life. Apart from the trauma, I feel safe with Evelyn and she's always fresh and exciting. My best recollections of intimacy are with her—though those types of moments are sadly unavailable to us now. I made an agreement with the universe that I would wait until I was ninety if I had to, but I would not settle before I found this significant other. If it meant I would never find this someone in my lifetime, then I would have been happy enough by myself. But for two flames who are never really apart...

CHAPTER 38

Reality Hits

Sometimes, to put everyone and everything around me and inside me out of misery, I feel so helpless I wish my brain would spontaneously blow out the side of my head as if a shotgun at short range had done the job. Sometimes I feel as helpless and worthless as a piece of low-quality shit—unsuitable even as fertilizer. I make myself small, close my eyes, and sincerely hope to disappear in a desperate attempt to spare others the great burden I am and to appease my inner critic who relentlessly provides ample proof that I am, in fact, a burden; and everyone, including myself, would be better off if I were gone. This is not a death-wish, not at all. My suicidal ideation is an urge from a sense of helplessness when there seems no other fix for the suffering I witness within myself and for the distress in others that I take on as my fault. My suicidal ideations come from a desire to care for the people I care about, even if it means relinquishing them of the burden of myself, regardless of how much I would like them in my life. Suicidal ideations are a personal reality that I have denied and kept to myself my whole life. I've learned this is a symptom of Complex Post Traumatic Stress Disorder (CPTSD) and that at certain times in my life, suicidal ideation has served an important function for survival in my environment, much as dissociative amnesia has.

Not all too surprisingly, it was my relationship with Evelyn that prompted and intensified my emotional flashbacks, leading me to undertake EMDR therapy. Suicidal ideations are one thing, hitting myself in the face is another. Since both are unacceptable and embarrassing, I needed extra treatment with Noah. Once I started these sessions, my repressed memories seeped in slowly at first, but after four sessions they flooded in fast. The recollections surged in from long ago and caused my

CPTSD symptoms to worsen. On the surface, however, I appeared fine, even to myself. I was effectively hiding this internal pain in front of Noah, though it was not my intention to have done so. It was no surprise, therefore, that he did not respond to my simmering crisis. I didn't fool Evelyn though; she detected this old staple for survival in me and emailed Noah to make sure he knew what was happening. This time he did respond, and immediately. After Evelyn's email, Noah called me. He was unusually panicked and was apologizing to me, but I was not sure why. I gathered from our conversation that he and Evelyn were worried and he suggested that I enter a specialized program for additional support. I took this all seriously and became open to intensive trauma work and learning about Dialectical Behavior Therapy (DBT).

Initially off-put by DBT because some of its core philosophies parallel Beescrit principles for mind control, I now recognize DBT as a way for me to deconstruct not only the cult's lies but my mother's too. I discovered more about DBT through personal study: It is an evidence-based psychotherapy treatment developed by psychology researcher, Marsha M. Linehan. DBT is used to increase cognitive and emotional regulation skills for those with addictive disorders, PTSD, personality disorders, eating disorders, and more.

By recognizing how truly traumatized I am and accepting this evidence-based reality, I can no longer excuse my abusers. My first partial day treatment program, heavily laden with DBT, helped me to begin accepting reality. By accepting my reality, I eased my fear of the flashbacks that were sprouting within me, allowing a sense of my inner Self to surface, albeit incrementally. It was DBT that framed the flashbacks of my experiences during birth and infancy—the harsh reality of which caused an early and initial onset of my dissociation for decades to come. DBT uncovered the shocking new information that lent cohesion and rationality to my life. I arrived at a reconciliation of the duality within me to understand why I could feel more than one way at once: anger and tenderness, love and betrayal, freedom and entrapment. Without an integration and acceptance of these paralleled opposing forces, I could not see the big picture and had remained trapped in blaming and punishing myself for the actions of my illness.

I was thirty-five years old. I recount an episode that occurred eight weeks after my dissociative amnesia began clearing. Its details trace the onset of the experience, its physical effects, and my implementation of the therapy techniques that equipped me to cope with as well as combat the trauma.

My guts twist in knots and I have bad gas pains—a typical spasm I frequently had to endure for as long as I can remember until I was twenty years old. I head up to the bathroom, I think so anyway, but go into the bedroom instead. I crawl on the bed on my side atop a white duvet with tiny mustard colored flowers. My guts relax as I breathe, and then I feel I am going to have a heart attack. Maybe for real. That my heart should suddenly stop truly seems possible because it is beating so consistently fast and hard, maybe since far before I first perceived it. *Heart rate may drop to zero.*

I am gripped with terror. I identify the fear and recognize there is no way out of it. On the bed curled in a fetal position, I close my eyes and tiptoe slightly back from the edge of the petrified part inside me, as I learned to do in therapy. With only a sliver of space between me and the precipice, I creep towards the kind, gentle, and curious parts of my nature—the way Noah coached me. I remember the hard truths from the trauma program that the therapist Clara presented to me earlier that afternoon, and I further brace myself for the onslaught of intense moments that will follow.

I mutter at first, after a few sharp, nearly silent sobs, "I've got you." That feels pretty good so I say it aloud again, a bit more robustly, "I've got you."

I repeat it in my mind but find myself slipping, so I tell myself different versions of similar sentiments aloud, "You are not alone. I am with you."

No heart rate dropping to zero?

It hurts, what I feel inside, nearly unbearable and yet soul-suckingly familiar; most of me is frozen, but the sound of my own voice grounds and soothes me. I begin accepting the pain, welcoming it, and most importantly, validating it. My heart continues pounding hard at an unnerving speed. I know I need to move from the bed, so I ask the petrified part of myself what it wants or needs. I listen, and it plays me a consoling melody.

I sit up from the bed and casually and obliquely let Evelyn know my state of affairs so as not to cause her too much concern. I escape her notice with subtlety. I have communicated and Evelyn knows to calmly keep her distance. I then pace around the kitchen and Evelyn starts cooking our dinner. I know I am still in a tight spot and my heart is pounding, that I need next to conjure up all my skills to regulate my emotions, but my abilities are limited. *What skill next? Phone a friend? Scary. Phone a friend. Tell him you can't really talk because you are overwhelmed but have some questions you'd like to ask him for perspective... Bingo! Hurry up and write down those questions before you forget!* I do it.

I bundle up for the winter weather and practically set up camp in my neighbor's shed—what I lovingly call my homeless shanty. It has an overhang so I can sit under there, smoke a cigarette, and phone a friend while watching the snow fall. My old beach buddy John doesn't answer my phone call. Now what am I going to do? Surely the cigarettes aren't helping, but my heart pounds just the same. I ponder if my life will be shortened by the amount of time my heart has been completely overactive. I remember the melody that the petrified part inside me wants to hear, so I start looking for the song. *Simon and Garfunkel, for sure, Live in New York 1967, Benedictus?* The moment I press play I know it is the wrong track. *Blessed, then?* It plays but that isn't it either. Then I put on *You Can't Always Get What You Want* by The Rolling Stones. *Ah, yes! This will do.* I listen, the choir sings gently in my ears at first. The guitar strums on the right and the French horn comes in from the left...

My mind recedes back to Noah and Clara. Clara, whom I knew for less than a total of four hours, did something for me in our afternoon session that I now witnessed unfurling before my eyes, but I cannot fathom its magnitude. I still don't know how Clara did what she did, but this is what it was like:

Clara spent a lot of time with me to get me to 'normalize' my experiences. To some extent, it was reasonable to believe that I was a lost cause, even though I'm not and we both knew that. She saw my great denial and protective parts and stared me kindly and directly in the face, but not too much, just discreetly enough for me to be curious what it would be like to let down my guards. Clara's pointed questions were drawing out the hard truths. She asked if doctors or teachers or family members or friends ever expressed concern about me or my brothers. I said no, but maybe, nothing that I could recall. Clara literally spelled things out for me like: D-S-S. I noted aloud that the word 'criminal' came to mind, and Clara did not belittle the association of the term. Clara matter-of-factly described what the function of the Department of Social Services (DSS) is as well as the common misconceptions about it. Clara often gently reminded me of the seriousness of my circumstances and guided me back towards myself each time I habitually deflected away any possible penetration into my reality with minimizations or jokes. Before we had finished our afternoon meeting, Clara reiterated that this was a venture into scary territory. I didn't know what she meant right then, but I was coming to an understanding.

Meanwhile, I return to my physical self and take stock:

Under the awning of my beloved homeless shanty in my neighbor's shed, my heart still pounds unnervingly fast. I have thus far successfully communicated with Evelyn, decided my next coping skill, and failed to reach my friend in a phone call. Next, my petrified self finds the melody it seeks for comfort and meaning. As I listen to the main vocals, reality percolates inside me; the music orchestrates an openness and I let my mind unfurl to the rhythm and lyrics. *I accept my mother for what she is. This is both sad and scary...* And then, my Self is revealed to me, and I feel it for the first time in decades. I cry old tears, smile, and laugh to jubilation. My mind shows me a view from the handlebars of my racing bicycle. I feel as if I am flying and the sensation of freedom is heavenly.

In retrospect, I did for myself in that moment what Clara had done for me earlier—I looked directly at myself. Next, memories of my brother Jack flood my mind. *I feel him in the flesh—his skin and bones, I smell him, and I hear his voice. I remember how much I love him. I realize how traumatized I am and that Jack must also be. What Jack thinks or how he feels when I'd completely FORGOTTEN our lives together are now an enigma to me.*

I remind myself to pace myself with the flood of visions and sensations coming at me. With that, my cognizance returns: I am in the backyard, the dog next door is barking, and I realize that I have just definitely cried and laughed without reserve. The best part is, I truly don't care if anyone heard me! I *need* this experience. I focus back on The Rolling Stones song and muse, *Yes! It's not my favorite part yet! Wait, is it? Do I hear the piano?! Not yet!*

I sit back in my seat with a certain freedom, relieved to have retrieved my Self even for a brief moment. My heart still pounds. The process is equal parts pain and savory connectedness. I try to keep pacing in my mind to the rhythmic presence of the music. Here come the piano and the uninhibited joyful screams of the choir at minute 6:34 of the track to which I completely surrender my heart. The song is over and my half-smoked cigarette is burnt out. No, "You can't always get what you want… but if you try sometimes, you just might find, you get what ya NEED!" and I needed to go eat dinner and be an adult with Evelyn.

Special thanks to Noah for steadfast and kind direction, as well as much needed comfort; and thanks to Clara for turning on the lights. I couldn't have survived this ordeal without either of you.

CHAPTER 39

Bad Case of Loving You

I call John my *man of God.* I met John on the beach years ago, battling myself with a beer buzz. I had a feeling I would meet a weirdo, and there he was, John. Making my way down from the dunes after having relieved myself of beer, I spied Mr. Cool with the shades, sun-kissed, confidently lounging in the sand, a plainly seasoned beach-goer.

I had passed him on my way up to the dunes and upon my return he inquired in a totally tubular tone, "You were here last Wednesday with your friends, weren't you?"

I turned, having already scurried past him as nonchalantly as I could.

"I like your music," John said.

Intrigued by the solid compliment, I replied, "Yeah, that was me."

Immediately regretting having responded, I thought, *Oh no, this is the strange man I knew I would meet today.* I invited John to join me at the side of my beach fire, promptly condemning myself for being too friendly while walking back to my beach spot. John later joined me by the fire.

Turns out John is an awesome dude and I like him. We do not see each other much, but we do speak with some regularity in quality discussions about life.

In 2019 during the Trump-Biden presidential election race, John told me, "I am losing all my friends, Vada. You are one of the only ones left and definitely one of the best."

John and I have a relationship in which we can talk about and explore almost any topic. John is well-versed in the Bible, by choice, not upbringing, and I truly enjoy hearing about things from a Biblical perspective. It gives me a new eye, even when I do not agree. John tells stories of the Bible in ways new to me; he does not shove them down my throat by any means, but to a good listener he can elaborate upon the Good Book's stories until the cows come home. John is knowledgeable, open, and most impressively, vulnerable.

John supported me when those nearest me couldn't bear my burdens, and he provided safety in the times I needed it. He probably doesn't know how he has protected me, but he has. He has cried with me and is the friend I had wanted to talk to on the night that I sat under the awning of my neighbor's shed. After my reality had hit me that night in the shed, reeling with questions about mental health, I eventually caught up to my buddy and spoke with him. John helped me flesh out some perspectives on mental illness and, in turn, how I relate to the traumatic experiences of my life and their effects on me as I operate in the world and in relationships. We spoke of Grace and me. I've got a bad case of loving my mother. I do not think I can be shaken from this love because it is based in biology. It is sad though, to love someone I know will hurt me.

A desire to understand this compelled me. John and I spoke about mental illness from the perspective of the Bible, a big topic in religious communities apparently. Our conversation defined the concept in which God "hardens the hearts" of his chosen people who are repetitively deceitful, manipulative, and cruel. I wondered, *is hardening of the heart an accurate metaphor for mental illness, and if so, then what about innocent humans affected by the hardened hearts of others? And is it natural for people to act meanly and crazy for no reason, especially towards innocent others?* Hearts must be hardened because it gets harder and harder for people to hold onto the goodness in their nature the more they are subjected to oppression through abuse and trauma in their various forms. Nature is fair, but this did not seem fair. Innocent others are harmed by those with hardened hearts. The punishment did not make sense relative to an all-loving God, but the sentiment felt loosely valid. John led me to the clarity I was searching for while navigating this maze of thought following a major emotional flashback I had experienced:

It was a bad one. It was the closest I'd ever come to suicide. Evelyn and I were engaged in the winding spiral of communication dictated by her trauma-brain when dissociation intruded upon me like a military attack, a common occurrence while my amnesia was first clearing. I tried to remain engaged in the dialogue while my brain was under siege. I suddenly found myself overtaken by a barrage of shrapnel-like, scattered flashbacks. I was fighting not to seem indifferent to Evelyn. It was like tracking my allies on my left flank and the enemy encroaching on my right. I couldn't manage the double processing with the impending threat of airstrikes. My brain inexplicably kept jumping through time and space with intense images, emotions, and physical sensations. It was like my sweet and passionate girl Evelyn was crying out to me as the enemy whisked me away captive to another terrifying time and place. I was seized by another series of flashbacks. I got very angry with myself afterwards. Suicidal ideations rose and then turned to combat strategy. I called Noah to the rescue.

In the wake of this emotional flashback I pondered: *Grace lost her mind. When? Don't know, but it happened. And here I am dealing with the repercussions of Grace's inadequate coping skills. Was Grace born with an unhealthy brain? If so, why? And why didn't Grace get the care she needed? If Grace was born healthy, then what happened to her and why? What hardened her heart? Why did Grace fall through the cracks?* These questions stretched my mind and revealed a far larger picture of society than I had expected. I had to zoom way way out to pan the scape.

I felt helpless, as I tended to, during and after stressful flashbacks. These questions harmonized with my helplessness when my mind suddenly revealed an answer to the Biblical question I'd posed to John about the innocent victims of hardened hearts: *I am not alone*. It clicked. Innocent victims of hardened hearts are fair game in nature because we are all a part of nature. It's the circle of life. It is all fair game: what we choose we get back, since we are ultimately inseparable in the eyes of mother nature. Oppression and trauma and their effects do not discriminate, presenting themselves on both sides of the coin from the homeless streetwalking mumbler to the politician publicly inciting a riot on his own nation's capital building. In order to cope with inner pain, it does not take a lifetime of abuse to become capable of violence or suicide or to become the walking dead. I think mental illness would present itself in other species if those decided to be cruel to their own kind; their hearts and minds would also get broken.

Grace grew up in a working poor sector of society, leaving her vulnerable to mental illness due to both social oppression and generational trauma. I, the daughter, inherited the effects of my mother's oppression and trauma through neglect and abuse, though my childhood environment was more privileged and therefore technically more 'secure' than hers. This ignorant cruelty is applied and sustained by generations of our own kind without considering that the repercussions are akin to dumping trash into our communal life-giving water supply. Generational trauma and social oppression are so ordinary that they penetrate like a dirty washcloth into the fabric of society, laundering hatred and crimes against humanity on an endless spin cycle.

CHAPTER 40

Inconveniently Interpersonal

While pondering perpetuated mental illness caused by generational trauma and social oppression, my symptoms of Complex Post Traumatic Stress Disorder didn't quit and the flashbacks persisted. Flashbacks are my brain's way of providing me information that was previously repressed by my greatest coping skill, dissociative amnesia. My flashbacks are often largely dissociative because that was the original experience—the disconnected dissociation buried itself deeply in the dark recesses of my memory. The concept of 'self' was absent—a common consequence of neglect or abuse in the early years of a human being's development. Beescrit Books fostered my eradication of my own 'self' too, so of course that environment had fit me like a glove. Since all brains have the capacity to manifest 'self', I am able to build a sense of self as an adult under the right care, though it is painstaking work. Sometimes a certain stimulus will bring on flashbacks, like a scent or a sound; sometimes they seem to come out of nowhere. My trauma is inconveniently interpersonal, so it makes sense as to why my mind associates experiences from long ago with the dearest relationship of all, my partnership with my often wildly expressive girlfriend Evelyn. Once, a conversation with Evelyn regarding some work I had to do sent me into a trauma response. I exiled myself to the basement to keep Evelyn safe from being disturbed or distressed by its occurrence. I was in a flashback that would last for several hours. Because it was really intense and I was dissociating a ton, I jotted down a few notes lest I should forget the incident: *Don't forget—tough time today in basement. I finally care if I die. Window crawling in and out— What was there? Hiding. Trauma response, hiding. Hearing shoes and wanting to crawl into cabinet. Remembering house.*

Brother. Looking at my eyes crying, how can anyone be okay with that? So many parts. So many parts. Don't forget. Mom taught me to treat her how she wanted me to, which worked out for me in many cases for surviving unsafe environments.

Parts of me are fractured, frozen in time and trapped in trauma. It is not as weird as it sounds. Everyone has parts. For example, someone may be excited to visit a friend they haven't seen in some time, while another part of them is dreading seeing that friend's annoying spouse during the visit. My parts are a bit more defined and intrusive. The brunt of the work for improving my CPTSD symptoms and what facilitates the safe integration of memories is syncing the fractured parts of myself. Most people's parts are synced by the natural conductor of a person's internal orchestra (their 'selves') while I must create a conductor where there has never been one. There are parts of me that do not feel safe, which is hopefully understandable after what I have experienced in my life—because mental health stigma is real and I did nothing to deserve such a state of being. As I learned in therapy, I logically and emotionally visit the 'part' of me who feels she needs to curl into a ball on the couch under blankets in the basement away from Evelyn because she had reminded me of work I had to get done with her usual high energy:

That part blamed Evelyn: *"She doesn't care about me. Why else would she pressure me to do work I didn't agree to do yet, 'Due ASAP!' especially with my history of people trying to control me?"*

But I gave *that* part of me the correct information: *"Evelyn **does** care about me, which is why Evelyn referred me to the job in the first place."*

Hmmm, okay, so this part of me now curled up on the couch should not blame Evelyn anymore because it now understands that Evelyn is not the issue in this case... And I recognize I was in a trauma response with *that* part of me out front and center. I had to superimpose this enlightened side of me onto *that* darkened side of me due to trauma. I immediately desired for Evelyn to know that my hiding was not about her. But I couldn't; I was too afraid. In the darkness of the basement undercover, my head was buzzing with fear and a constant jarring anticipation. Aware that sleeping is an avoidant behavior, I respected sleep as my skill for the moment. I hoped I would either fall asleep and Evelyn would go about her day, or if I stayed still long enough, Evelyn would realize my reaction had nothing to do with her personally. It was an issue far beyond her work referral on short notice. I was not tired; I just wanted time to pass without me present. I am not sure what was scaring me in the flashback. I slept for an hour and a half. When I came to, I listened for movement in the house. It was silent and I thought maybe Evelyn had gone out for the day. Uncertain and on edge, perfectly silent and still in the basement, I knew it was not Evelyn I was afraid of. I was still in a flashback. It was not remembering what had happened to me that made me so afraid and caused my intense internal confusion. I considered a better place to hide. *I have already retreated to the basement. Where is a better place to hide?*

I heard the floor above my head creak under Evelyn's footsteps. Listening intently, the scared part of me wanted to clear out the storage cabinet and squeeze myself inside between the shelves. Recognizing the strangeness of the inclination, I was able to stay curious about what was happening across my worlds.

Evelyn moved about the house. I wanted to find a better hiding spot or to go outside to hide. At this point, I am confined to the trauma experienced by *that* part of me. I plotted, *Okay, going out the slanted metal bulkhead doors could be an option, but a noisy one.* Further consideration led me to sneaking up the basement stairs in socked feet, across the kitchen, and out the back sliding door. Evelyn might hear the sliding door, but I would be hiding already on the side of the house if she looked for me. Still pondering escape routes, I realized the basement stairs creaked so loudly that I wondered how I would navigate this obstacle. I remembered scheming like this when I was younger and became encouraged that my legs were long now so I could scale the stairs in just three steps… And I realized again that I was still in a trauma response.

I texted Evelyn, even though we were both still home: OKAY, SO I HAVE A VERY VULNERABLE 'PART' HERE, PROMINENT IN MY PAST EXPERIENCE. I AM AFRAID AND DON'T WANT YOU TO SEE OR HEAR ME.

Evelyn texted back: WOULD IT BE HELPFUL IF I LEAVE THE HOUSE?

YES.

Once sure that Evelyn had left the house, I was able to make space between me and my experience of the scared and hiding part of me. My beloved therapist Noah had told me that when a 'part' appears, it either needs my help or wants to help me. I offered *that* young part of myself compassion. Though I could not specifically remember *that* young part's plight, I could feel it. I felt safe enough to cry.

My mind flooded with memories of family homes with more details filling in. There were many memories, but one particularly stood out:

I was a teenager climbing in and out of a window on the second floor farthest from Grace and Oskar's bedroom. I went out on the roof, down the ladder in the back of the house, and came back into the house the same way, as I sometimes would do. There was a bunch of shit in the hallway in front of the window that I had to climb over, and I remembered what the movements felt like in my body, but could not remember what objects were in front of the window. I desperately wanted to call Jack to make sense of the information but did not want to bring up potentially challenging memories for him with my inquiry. I was in no condition for managing that type of conversation, soupy with information across time and space. I remembered hiding fairly often, in clever places, and also hiding my brother.

I soothed myself, telling *that* part of me desperate to hide that *this* part of me was really sorry that *that* part at some time needed to function this way to survive. A waterfall of memories cascaded following my internal expression of compassion towards the younger version of myself. It was a lot. Hungry for answers and sensing that I had enough 'bandwidth' to allow the next wave of memories, I let them come. The process is trippy as my brain reveals information so obviously there. It's like a weird world with magic, not a safe place, but magic nonetheless. A washstand appeared in the hallway which had already revealed itself to me weeks before. Then, I got curious and wanted to know what was on the washstand, but I couldn't see, just as I could not see the washstand itself in the previous memory of the hall.

In real life, I went upstairs to the kitchen and then remembered looking at myself in the mirror when I was little, crying. I then went to a mirror outside of the kitchen and looked into my eyes. It was sad what I saw in my eyes but also beautiful. I saw the sweetness of my being beyond the sadness and fear in my eyes and all over my face. It occurred to me how often Grace saw the same face and gleefully kicked sand in it. While Owen was her 'golden child', Grace definitely did not care if she made me or Jack cry, pouring salt into the wounds. I remembered Jack crying and what he looked like, desperate. My automatic thought looking into my eyes in the mirror was, *What kind of a cruel person can do this to children and be okay with it?*

My mind still will not allow me to conjure up memories that might be too threatening or fearful to me. Maybe one day it will, maybe it won't. I don't think I need all the details. One might wonder why I was hiding with or without Jack, climbing through a window with or without objects in the way. *Welcome to my recovery from amnesia.* I cannot always put all the pieces together in my puzzle. My memory of missing moments. Remembering is part of the process. I do not force or impede the process except when my system is too weak and sensitive to bear it. During those moments, I employ coping strategies to safely move out of trauma responses until I am ready to experience what my system is hankering to communicate and process. In a sense, I have to create within myself the secure attachment that is usually acquired during the natural course of development. It is a shit ton of work and I couldn't do it without professional support.

Evelyn is abundantly caring and does not abandon me. She often feels culpable that my experiences are her fault, and sometimes she does assist them. But I know she's not to blame. My internal system certainly blamed Evelyn for a moment though. Yes, I felt pressure from Evelyn due to regular old communication issues around work deadlines and there was compounded stress from our relationship dynamic present, but my reaction was not personal. My fear and hiding was relative to times past when I felt truly unsafe, times that I repress and need to heal in my brain. And I know that my battle is with myself. Evelyn merely brings to light what needs to be addressed and healed within me. I know I do the same for Evelyn too. *But two flames—we bring each other to the light through the darkness.*

CHAPTER 41

Revenge

The barely manageable barrage of flashbacks went on for weeks, maybe months. Eventually my left shoulder spasmed after an excessive bout of heart palpitations and writing with poor posture for too many hours. The pain was so bad I thought maybe I was dying. Losing sensation and strength in my arm and fingers, my shoulder and chest cramped from the inside in surges. I texted Merlin, my modern day version of an ancient medicine man. Merlin and I have worked together in various forms professionally and have become friends.

Merlin sees me in a deeper sense than most, though he rarely reveals his perceptions of people, until recently. I visited Merlin in my physical agony. Merlin surveyed my overall state by placing his fingers skillfully on my wrist. He likened the state of my body to someone recently released from prison, or having finished a vigorous regimen of chemotherapy. I was not surprised to hear the similes from Merlin.

Merlin always fixes me. I knew if anyone could help, or at least confirm I was dying that it would be Merlin. He confirmed I was *not* dying. Merlin primarily uses tiny needles to treat his patients. His vocation is based in eastern medicine, but he integrates a touch of the west. He is exceptionally skilled and I happen to respond especially well to his treatments. I really love Merlin. The phrase slips from my lips now and again by accident, aloud. I happen to like Merlin's character a whole lot too; which I can best describe as non-invasive, cool, steady, and surprisingly funny because Merlin takes his work very seriously. I told Merlin about my dissociative amnesia, frequent episodes of dissociation, flashbacks, nightmares, etc. and that I'd discovered that I'd been abused for most of my life and was now putting the pieces back together.

Merlin listened and later communicated, "Everyone has their path," and sincerely told me my path was meant for me.

I think that is true, no matter how fucked up it all has been. My pain was significantly reduced and I had more energy overall after my second treatment.

As I set about creating the illustration for the setting of the *Folklore* chapter in this book—it is of the house where most of the sexual abuse occurred with Babo—a thought about the various locations where I boarded with Beescrit dawned on me: I had lived in one state during my last year of service at Beescrit Books, and five years before that, I had worked under Cotton in two other states. That left me three years working under Babo. Three years. Longer than I had first realized.

I started piecing together the chronology:

For the first six-months, Babo prepped me, telling me things like, "You are a wild horse and I will break you."

I thought he meant my ego! Like, spiritually, karmically, or whatever. Babo transformed what he was doing to me into a favor for my spiritual growth. He had requested I get a physical exam and test for sexually transmitted diseases. He couldn't wait though: without a condom on a dark night before the results of the tests came back—it happened. Everyone else in the house was asleep. We were in the kitchen first, then it happened in the living room. Amidst creating the *Folklore* illustration of the house, I suddenly flashed back to the moment right before it had first happened. I thought: *I should have known something was wrong.* Babo made a point of mentioning that he had done it before the test results came back as an expression of trust. And then it went on for two years or longer. I don't remember most of this time span and hopefully I won't. Gross. I asked myself what

I would do if I could go back in time to the moment before anything had happened sexually with Babo. The answer scared me: *I'd blow his fucking brains out before I let him do any of what he did to me, especially right in the moment before he first truly crossed the line.* I felt sad. I cried hard because the answer scared me so much. I can barely stand a plant's suffering. I feel sad for bouquets of cut flowers, soothing myself with happy thoughts of how the cut flowers will make someone feel loved. How can this sort of loving person conclude that taking a life would be the best option? Well, it wouldn't only have been for me: it would have been for every other person Babo ever had mistreated and to stop him from doing it ever again.

I visited Merlin, and shared the clarified timeline of Babo's abuse. Merlin asked if it was a family member. I told him no and that I was twenty years old when it began. Merlin treated me. I rested in the private treatment room while the tiny needles penetrated my flesh to work their wonders. As I rested, the awful moment with Babo in the living room came to my mind again. The memory less shocking, I plotted my revenge more logically while in Merlin's serene clinic. Next surfaced in me the reality that Babo had been abused by his father; one of the Beescrit instructors had mentioned it. Taking respite in Merlin's clinic, the effects of generational trauma again revealed themselves to me. How can I *not* have compassion for Babo? I do not think I am capable of not feeling empathetic, regardless of Babo's cruel nature and what he has done to me. Babo is still a scumbag though and should probably be institutionalized.

Babo, Grace, and I are survivors of trauma and oppression, and there are countless others. Babo and Grace crossed the line and lost their humanity. I didn't. I cope differently. I do not believe Grace and Babo were born inherently inhumane, but they were vulnerable generationally and socially. Preventative measures are available to protect ourselves and our loved ones from the dire rippling repercussions of mental illness, more or less severe than depicted in this story. Meeting others with decent human relativity and making quality healthcare accessible are paramount to reducing this risk society creates for itself. Not everyone will be capable of respecting each other, but I think most of us are capable of courageous kindness and balanced respect in support of our collective well-being.

CHAPTER 42

Human Relativity

Despite Developmental Trauma, walking blindly with learned incessant amnesia to cope with the brutality I had faced at the hands of my mother and then Beescrit, good people saved me from becoming cruel by taking interest.

In originally defining human relativity I wanted to use the term *love,* but thanks to my fellow trauma therapy group member, I realized *love* is too precise. Love is not necessary for human relativity. Human relativity is looser than love, requiring less work, and less intensity. It is a baseline, staving off harmful states of mental illness among us. Experiences with other human beings need only not be shitty or terrifying to establish or reestablish effects of human relativity. The bar is low here; a kind "hello" counts. I propose human relativity as a preventive measure for mental illness, and therefore, for crimes against humanity. Why did I not turn to cruelty? Scientifically, it is rare for persons with severe, prolonged traumatic experiences to preserve goodness within themselves. I adhered to goodness because of Oskar's kindness, my connection with my brothers and grandparents, quality engagements with teachers and other adults, the company of good friends, and the safety of my neighborhood. Even when persons around me are dubious in integrity, my adeptness at creatively twisting the convolutions of liars into something positive also serves to keep me kind. Furthermore, my relationship with nature brings me the serenity that goodness sometimes requires.

I believe my brain did not turn to cruelty because I had received enough human relativity and safe social connection in my environment. *Thank goodness I was born into an economically privileged community where places and people are generally safer, huh? I'd probably be dead or institutionalized without that blessed component.*

As my amnesia continued clearing, I initiated communication with people whom my brain had largely repressed or abandoned. These same people who had given me human relativity when I was young, would in turn nurture me with it once again. Even without my full memory of them, it was natural for me to need to reach out to others from my earlier years with whom I'd felt safe. The details of our former bonds might have been weak and fuzzy to me but my feelings about them were strong and clear. One of my earliest ventures into this new territory grounded me with my old friend Vera.

Once Beescrit Books was ancient history, still adrift in amber bubbles, I contacted my old high school friend Vera. I didn't remember the details of our relationship yet, but I didn't need to. We reconnected so seamlessly that once my amnesia began clearing, I had no qualms about seeking her perspective about both my personal and familial past during our times together. The mere sound of her voice at once swathed me in a sense of my own security and a sense of her ringing sincerity— an equation that makes for certainty. She treated me exactly the same as always, and without my prompting, she reassured me that I was a good person by recalling our former time together.

Vera did her best to convince me that I am still one of the kindest people she has ever met. "Why else would I still talk to you after all this time? And even now, we just picked up from where we'd left off. Do you think my mother likes a lot of people?" Vera asked.

I chuckled at the truth and how much I love all that Vera is. I cried a short bit with Vera, expressing how much I love and appreciate her and that I remembered her now.

Vera told me not to doubt myself for a second, "You were good then and you are good now."

Vera informed me that I was highly sociable and that I always had money because I worked so hard. I was good to my friends, even ones who weren't good to me back, and I never seemed to care either way. She reminded me that I would call her on my way to somebody's house and ask if I could drop by for a visit even if it were a half-hour's drive out of my way. I'd go to Vera's house and talk with her and her parents who are apparently fond of me.

"Okay, I'm off to *so and so's*," I'd announce, and leave just as quickly as I'd come.

"Not everyone is like that, Vada," Vera told me.

Vera somewhat blamed herself for my disappearance. Come to find out, several people blamed themselves for whatever they thought had happened to me.

Vera said her mother would ask after me, "Have you heard from Vada? You should really call to make sure she is okay."

I remember Vera's mother now, her father too, and I love the whole family. Vera came to Beescrit Books For Wellness for a class when I had first joined. She smelled BS and moved along.

"You were too gullible," Vera said, adding, "Naive."

Vera apologized for her honesty, but honesty is exactly what I was seeking.

I asked Vera about her experience of Grace.

"I never saw her much. I saw your dad way more, like at your sporting events."

Vera explained I was always nice to Grace, but it was also clear my mother and I were not close. "Your mom had a friend who was always around though, and you seemed to like her," Vera said.

Vera had added this one unmistakable identifying marker, and I knew this had to be Jane.

I shared a draft of this book with Jane who confirmed that everything regarding my mother that I'd said about her and quoted from her was true. Jane said that she felt sad reading the contents of this book.

Mostly she wondered, "Where the hell was I?"

Jane is not one to buy bullshit, so she was additionally befuddled by how Grace managed to pull the wool over her eyes. A notch on Grace's narcissistic belt, winning over the woman nobody messes with. Jane and I are growing closer, or more precisely, unearthing our closeness. In some way, I feel Jane knows me better than I know myself. In another way, I feel Jane is getting to know the real me better as we sort through the pile of filthy falsehoods that Grace told Jane about me. The relationship can be fear-provoking at times, however, since Jane keeps in touch with her longtime friend Grace. Despite this, Jane has given me confidence in my story and has filled many important blanks for me; when my brain overwhelms me with doubt I draw strength from Jane's validation.

My experiences with Jane and Vera are hefty examples of human relativity. It is emotional for me to connect with people who did not disappear completely from my life, even some with whom I had recently spoken. My return to them in order to rekindle a relationship in the forgotten details of love or mutual affection was different for me because new bits of recollections made me curious about what else I didn't recall. There were many good memories that I had 'lost' while I was limited to detailed information that I needed for living in the present environment. Of course, these emotions loomed large in the presence of my family: Oskar, Jack, and Owen. *Sad to say again that Grace is a separate entity in this matter, as I mostly feel an unfathomable gripping fear that inhibits my breathing and no desire to connect with her.*

Most people I reconnected with have been happy to help me make sense of myself and I am abundantly grateful for their human relativity. Though the situation can get sticky for all of us, Oskar and Owen have been as supportive as I could ever ask for. Jack and I have a lot of work to do, but I am grateful that he is somewhat in my life. Evelyn puts up with a lot of shit from me in trauma responses and supports me real-time, and thankfully my symptoms are gradually lessening in their severity. Noah is a force. Evelyn and I often express our awe of Noah's capacity for steady quality mental health care. I met other fabulous professionals including Clara and a brilliant brain scientist. Several friends are also vital human relativists. Participation in weekly groups with other people who have trauma also supports my developmental recovery. *From the bottom of my heart, I thank all who supported me and gave me human relativity throughout my life and especially those of you who stepped up when I said such frightening words like 'abuse' and 'amnesia'.*

CHAPTER 43

ER

THANKS FOR THE DRESS

Suicidal ideations intensified as flashbacks continued to pummel me, between ten and fifty per day. Needing more professional support, I called my state health insurance. *Aaahhh, public healthcare.* The insurance representative advised me that the fastest and only way to go about getting the care I needed was to visit the emergency room. Turned out though, if I wanted an evaluation from my public health insurance provider to approve coverage for a higher level of care, I had to first agree to do whatever insurance decided before I knew what program or where. No, I was not allowed to research their decision and decide. If I did not want to be evaluated, I was free to go. I became willing to take on serious debt to get myself the care I needed and avoid a padded room; however, it became additionally apparent that because of my poor-person-status and public healthcare plan, paying privately for care is not allowed. If my public health insurance catches wind that I manage to pay the suffocating medical care debt, there could be serious repercussions—Where is that extra chunk of change coming from each month? I would be deemed ineligible for the public healthcare plan and possibly acquire more costs or charges.

I entered the lobby of the hospital ER and did the COVID dance. *You know how it goes.* The administrator gave me a bracelet with my name on it and I waited for the triage nurse, Casey. Casey was kind. I told her I would forget her name and I have. Casey explained I would be changing into a hospital gown and giving someone my belongings. I also peed in a cup, all routine. There was a security officer stationed outside my door. High-nerved coming into the hospital and in triage with Casey, I was out of it. I barely moved a muscle once in the hospital room.

I sat cross-legged slumped on the hospital bed, wiped out, really looking like I truly belonged there.

The security guard was very nice, a middle-aged gentleman who brought me a warm blanket right away. The next person I met was a woman who wanted answers to A, B, and C questions, Amy. My eyes teared up while mentioning that Grace knew I was in a cult and left me there.

Amy wasn't interested in my actual experience: "We won't go into specifics now. The medical doctor and behavioral health social worker will both be in to speak with you."

After I completed the questionnaire, Amy said, "Well, I don't think they'll take you into a treatment program based on what you have told me," and left the room.

I was immediately at a loss, realizing my chances of getting the care I needed covered by insurance was slim to none. I cried for myself and every other person like me, perfectly good people who cannot get the help they need to live fully in this world because of the elusively complicated and broken system. I asked Amy to please call Noah, my therapist, and Amy agreed.

The next person who came to see me was the medical doctor, Dr. Henry. He asked me what was going on. I told Dr. Henry most pressing was my fear of not getting the help I needed in order to live a good life. I was embarrassingly emotional expressing my fear. I might as well have been rocking back and forth in a straight jacket. Dr. Henry listened to me and then told me there were three ways my visit could conclude. He wasn't sure which way it would go for me, but he was going to check my lungs and listen to my heart. Dr. Henry left after listening to my lungs and heart with a stethoscope. In the doorway Amy appeared as she stood between me and the security officer. She iterated it was unlikely I would be approved for higher level care through my insurance.

I clarified with Amy, to be sure I understood correctly: "I could either A: go home, or B: section myself into an unknown system of care. If I chose option B, I would be moved by ambulance to a place of the system's choosing and I could not change my mind once I chose option B?"

Amy confirmed that I understood correctly.

"Please excuse me," I said, fucking scared shitless, "but this is bullshit. I am not frustrated with you, but I am very angry for myself and people like me who do not have access to the care they need."

I looked away from Amy and thought to myself: *Just because I am not bouncing off the walls and acting like a crazed lunatic, I cannot get an appropriate higher level care? What does the system need? For my symptoms to worsen until I make an actual suicide attempt so the public health padded room would make more sense? Don't we want to avoid that?*

I stifled my anger and looked at Amy again, "What did Noah say?"

Amy's reply informed me that Noah had done his best but had no power in the situation. I asked to speak with Noah. The hospital staff got a battery-powered phone from another floor because the phone jack was removed from the room I was in. I wanted to confirm my inclination with Noah that option B was scary as sin. What a fucking sick joke and a complete waste of everyone's time.

A mute Asian kid rested in a bed outside my hospital room door. He would not speak. I was not surprised when Emily, the kind nurse in purple pants, gently told me they needed to clear the room and get it ready for the next person. We were interrupted by none other than Poppy, the behavioral health social worker for whom I'd been waiting. Poppy, who was very busy, asked me no questions about my behavioral health at all. Poppy never even looked me in the eye, but she hurried off to print my discharge paperwork. Another nurse came in and asked if Emily in the purple pants had finished speaking with me, softly reinforcing that I needed to get out.

Standing in the obscenely bare room—especially for the crazies in a hospital gown—and changing back into my street clothes while Emily changed the bed linens, Poppy came back and handed me the discharge paperwork.

"I am writing a book," I stated in a clear tone, intending for my volume to rise above the bustle. It did the trick. Poppy looked at me and I added, completely aware of how insane I was about to sound, "One day you may read my book and say to yourself, 'Holy shit!' this person came through my ER."

It was too good a moment to pass up so that I could write this very paragraph and possibly make a connection with Poppy, but I would not be surprised if she barely remembers the interaction. She, unfazed; I, invisible. On my way out of the ER, I saw two young nurses in the hallway. I tried to give them my hospital gown and blanket. I ended up taking the items home and photographing the attire on my neighbor's clothesline. Hopefully, I will never find myself in an emergency room in the same capacity.

I texted Oskar to let him know I'd gone to the emergency room. Oskar encouraged me to move along. I knew Oskar did not understand how much I needed help, or the fact that my troubles had nothing to do with wallowing in the past. I was going to need more professional help. My dedication to therapy and doing all I could on my own to manage my symptoms were not enough, and I was unable to function. I was distracted by flashbacks and was mostly dissociating, apart from enduring nightmares during which I yelled out, loudly and clearly enough that on a different floor of the house Evelyn could and did transcribe what I called out in my sleep. At worst, continuing after the futile ER visit, my suicidal ideations were rising and intensifying.

I was on the edge and needing more help at my visit to the ER. Oskar's well-intentioned encouragement for me to move on stirred a terror in me that I would not be able to speak with him anymore because our realities were too different. Oskar could not understand that my experience was not a choice. I knew Oskar wanted to support me, but I also saw the possible end of my relationship with my father. A Hail Mary in its own right, I asked if Oskar would be willing to participate in a family therapy session. He said yes.

Oskar met me and Noah in a therapy session after my visit to the emergency room. Thank goodness Noah is who he is. Noah's passion, caring, knowledge, and sense of urgency shone through in a big way. Oskar was persuaded to give me access to the additional care I need since I cannot do it myself from my place in society. Oskar doesn't understand what he is doing for me exactly, but he is giving me a second chance at life. Life will still be hard, as life is, but it will be a more fair fight if I can calm the fuck down and create a sense of 'self' through the correct care without financial stress exacerbating it.

Doubled over in the backyard near my neighbor's clothesline, I clutched my stomach as it spasmed. It is only because Oskar is willing to help me that I have hope. This cold truth sickened me personally and socially. I found myself again entirely reliant on someone besides myself and it scared me, but what really twisted me up was the thought of people trapped in oppression and trauma who do not have an Oskar to pull them from the trenches. People who are socially oppressed are often dismissed, deemed menaces of society or "crazy" for what are literally their survival skills and coping mechanisms of the brain. They most often do not have access to the healthcare they need to get better—they are trapped as I would have been if Oskar were unwilling to help me—and left increasingly vulnerable to more severe symptoms of mental illness which is no good for society. Those wounded by a broken social system bring to light a large social issue, but it has been our collective tendency to point fingers at them and condemn them for not improving their impossible circumstances. I cried for at least an hour over the realization in private, on and off, with another long forty-minute stretch of tears before I was able to go to bed and sleep.

CHAPTER 44

Pissed Off

My visit to the ER left me pissed off at white people. I posited the inequality of the healthcare system squarely on the shoulders of the white race. *Was I a racist? Not by nature. If anyone could tolerate people's—any people's—shortcomings and differences, it was I.* No, my rage was about power—the power certain people indiscriminately wield over others. And it is systemically penetrated into our entire culture, both American and global: micro and macro systems in society from families to government.

With my introspection about my prejudice, I asked myself how I could reasonably relate to people of Asian descent. Because when I spot a middle-aged Asian man resembling Babo, from a place beyond rationale or logic I am inclined to punch the guy in the face or run him over with my car—a natural response considering my experience with middle-aged Korean males. When I spot a Cotton lookalike, I often want to hide or run away or yell at her. Thankfully, I only observe these responses within myself and do not act on them. It is merely a trained and primal instinct to safeguard myself in such encounters. If Koreans were a known threat to the safety of my own community and if I had less human relativity, my reflexive fear and anger might yield to more harrowing behaviors for self-protection. I have no personal problem with strangers of Asian descent and there are plenty of Asian people whom I very much like, but I still need to cope with my biological reactions. Because I'd be most vulnerable to suspicion of Koreans or Asians due to Beescrit, and because I have suffered my own mental health issues from abuse, my sensitivities are heightened, and though I am not perfect, my defenses are fortified against falling into the trap of the socially systemic norms of power and even my own biological 'prejudices'. The compulsion to share this awareness is so strong in me that I had to tell my story.

I was tempted to forgo writing this book once I started to get the healthcare I need, which speaks to how easy it is to remain comfortable, forget about others, and keep on keepin' on in a broken system that endangers precious lives. But then I linked up with my friend Maeve.

Serendipity! It was like a calling for me to undertake a crusade. We had crossed paths at alcohol recovery meetings. Twice Maeve had approached me after hearing me speak at meetings and encouraged me to write. Maeve thought I had a knack for storytelling and gave me her phone number. I finally contacted her once I commenced writing. Maeve informed me that she also suffered from flashbacks, dissociation, and amnesia due to abuse; and she happened to be a writer as well. Maeve has connections to the world of privilege and healthcare as I do. Our mutual amnesia and passion for writing morphed into a simpatico friendship. It is rare to find functioning sober survivors of our type, so our connection is quite extraordinary. I was inspired to keep writing.

When reality hit me upside the head and my memories started flowing in, I was compelled to write, and then write some more. I couldn't hold a conversation, but I was creatively writing my face off. As my writing accumulated and my symptoms slowly subsided, I resorted to my new-found friend Maeve for her invaluable encouragement and guidance.

CHAPTER 45

Privilege and Fragility

MY BROTHER OWEN AND ME

this guy is a miracle
I am so proud of him

OWEN

Along with privilege comes a fragility fast upon it. The two hold hands. When I discovered I was in a position to speak about the effects of oppression and trauma, I had accessed privileged healthcare which granted me comfort in the ability to move on. I am not fragile because I can accept the unbelievable accounts of the oppressed and traumatized. I don't doubt oppressive or traumatic stories because I have my own. Privileged persons sometimes cannot relinquish their impersonally clean and clear stance on oppression or trauma and often further fly into a tirade on the topics, a tirade riddled with uninformed opinion. When privileged opinion is confronted with facts on oppression, then a fragility can present itself, shattering privileged people like glass. The word fragility is an apt one because the privileged people's world is shaken by the durable facts; these individuals fight to keep their reality from splitting so as to maintain their virtuous beliefs on oppression and preserve their peace of mind.

I was on the phone with Owen, my youngest brother. Owen brought up the use of they/them/their pronouns being integrated into elementary school curriculums.

Owen asked, "Shouldn't gender identity be talked about in sex education in the fifth grade?" I knew right away Owen was lacking correct information.

"Gender identity is not about sex. Why would you suggest it be addressed in sex education class?" I asked Owen.

"Because it is too much for little kids to try to learn. They are just figuring out how to form sentences still, using he and she pronouns, why further confuse them?"

I told Owen it may be one of those times we agree to disagree.

I let Owen off the hook. I was not particularly in the mood to deeply dive into the issue of gender identity and equality anyway, but Owen was very curious, and Grace taught me to never look a gift horse in the mouth. Owen is a great person to talk to about social justice and equality because I know Owen, like so many compliant oppressors, is not prejudiced. Compliant oppressors are people who oppress others, often by accident, based on publicly ingrained misinformation and inherited generational influences, not necessarily on their nature. If Owen understood, he would never suggest it was not a good idea to integrate proper use of all gender identity pronouns into elementary school curriculums.

Turns out, Owen is not fragile.

He prodded me, "Vada, you mean to tell me if it were your kids, you'd be cool with them changing their gender identity?"

I replied, "Yes, Owen, I would support my kids in knowing themselves and how they identify with themselves and the world. It is a process. I was at a gay pride parade once where I saw people in various phases of their gender expression, feeling out what was right for them. It looks strange sometimes, but it is a process, and not an easy one."

Owen was silent.

I explained to Owen that it sucks when you do not feel right inside yourself. If you are born in a body you do not identify with then language is only a start. I began sharing my personal experience as a gay woman and formerly gay child, who has personally considered her gender identity.

"Come on, Vada," Owen interrupted dismissively with a tinge of hope, "you were fine," he said.

"I was not fine Owen. I did things I would not have done that were not good for me. I was in danger many times, for many reasons, but consideration of my identity would have been valuable, in a healthy environment or not, and definitely as an adult."

After coming out, I considered my gender identity several times. I accepted I was a woman for most of my life and settled the issue of gender identity when I was pushing age thirty. Conveniently, my gender identity is female.

Owen agreed it would have been safer if I had identified my gender earlier in my life and then my sexual orientation, but his festering misunderstanding cracked a joke, "If you're going to be a man, okay! If you're going to be a woman, okay. It's all good to me, just get to it."

"Sadly, it is not that easy, Owen," I said.

Owen asked, "Well, what do you mean? Just go to the doctor…"

I interrupted, "Many people do not have access to care and definitely not to specialized medical care."

Owen, still on the fence, added, "People do it wrong, they need to be psychologically evaluated."

I concurred that people in gender transition should be evaluated psychologically for safety in their process and told Owen of the extended dangers for people forced to find treatments and hormones on the street with no access to medical care.

"Oh, my gosh," Owen said quickly with clarity and enthusiasm, "This should be covered by Medicare and Medicaid!"

Relieved, I exclaimed, "Yes, Owen! It absolutely should; that is quite right."

Language is only a start towards social acceptance, safety, and wellness for certain people; never mind, the additional medical care and procedures some people need. Owen now has correct information and understands the importance of integrating a use of they/them/their pronouns to elementary school curricula for those identifying outside gender norms of male and female. However, if Owen had not been both honest and willing to listen, or if he had insisted on his own thoughts on the topic with which he has no personal experience, the understanding could not have occurred. In other words, if Owen were fragile instead of curious, the conversation could not have happened. I think most compliant oppressors are like Owen, not actually prejudiced, but imprecisely informed as intended by the system.

CHAPTER 46

You Don't Know Jack

ME AND MY BROTHER JACK

People who are oppressed and traumatized are easily and often discredited for a variety of reasons. It can be unbearable hearing a story about the agonizing experiences of a stranger, let alone about those of someone you know, maybe more so if the person's story somehow hits home with you personally. I had been avoiding Grace altogether in conversations with my brothers, even before the amnesia broke. Bursting with love for Jack when my amnesia was first clearing, I initially went to him in hopes he could detail the happy times we had together, but I spoke around my mental health and my mother. I sought only to nurture my connection with my long lost brother. About a year after my amnesia broke, I spoke with Jack on the telephone. At this point I had decided I could not, with any level of self-respect, engage with my mother, and had halted all communication with her. Nothing seemed to happen when I did this—the holidays passed and so did Grace's birthday without a word from me; and by the way, I received no word from her either. Jack's lips may have occasionally reported some of my mother's fury towards me along with her dismissal of any truths I had disclosed about her.

My relationship with my brother Jack is very important to me and I had disappeared from Jack's life for many years. Because of this, I try to be as present with him as much as I can. We spoke on the phone for an hour and a half. We were reminiscing about old video games and cartoons. Then he brought Grace up out of nowhere. He may have been a little drunk, but I am not sure.

Jack launched into a harangue of criticism, insisting: "Vada, you need to resolve your issues with mom. Your memories are bullshit. They are not even your own memories, they are other people's memories, or just stories other people told you about. What did mom actually do to you? She was a good mom and she loved us! The therapists are filling your head with nonsense, misinformation! What is your therapist's name? Tell me! They need to hear the other side of the story. I won't talk to you again if you don't allow me in on a therapy session so I can set the record straight."

I actually desperately wanted to remember more of the good times, but that didn't seem possible because he was yelling at me. And there is a part of me that really wants to be wrong about everything, but the proof is in the pudding.

Evelyn appeared, who could hear Jack yelling at me through my padded headphones. Eye contact with her grounded me. I tried to tell Jack how our mother knew I was in a cult and left me there.

"They were a TEAM!" Jack snapped at me, though the 'team' had been dismembered when I was twenty years old, exactly the time I started slathering myself in Beescrit. "Dad is a smart man. You think he didn't know you were in a cult? We ALL knew you were in a cult."

I told Jack that our father did not know Beescrit Books was a cult and that I didn't know it was a cult either.

"I am smart too," I said.

He concurred and spat, "But if you blame one parent, you have to blame the other!"

It was like he was Grace's megaphone. I tried telling Jack about some of the memories from when I was a baby, like when I was left alone for God knows how long and my experience of crying and dissociating as an infant. *I admit that does sound a little crazy, especially when said aloud, but it is the only truth I have.*

His heart burned with fiery exasperation. "You think dad would let that happen? How could that have happened?" he sharply responded.

I nervously replied, "No, I don't think dad would let that happen. I just think the neglect happened enough to do some serious damage to my development."

Jack laughed and mocked me, "Oh, so you can't remember anything, but now you can remember when you were a baby and even the difference between night and day, weekends and weekdays? You've hit your head too many times, Vada—in car accidents and with drugs and alcohol."

His enraged insistence that hitting my head too many times was the cause of my amnesia was very painful for me to hear, especially coming from him.

I couldn't believe how calm I stayed on the phone with him, though I did have some suicidal ideations rise and I certainly was mildly dissociative as Jack bombarded me for twenty minutes straight calling me crazy and delusional. I couldn't bring myself to hang up on him so I tried explaining a bit more. When I presented instances of Grace physically abusing me, Jack said that I was the one who provoked Grace to hit me and bang my head against the wall. He insisted that he and I were the bad ones, and that Grace was showing us 'tough love' in her reactions to our 'bad behavior'. These sentiments rang an old familiar bell in me.

Unfortunately, the conversation caused me to lose trust in Jack, but I understood where he was coming from. If Jack were to accept my reality it would mean accepting his own and I certainly knew how painful that process was. I had avoided it like the plague and practically moved to another planet, instead. The denial is staunchly dense and for good reason—the truth is too much to confront.

A couple of days later Oskar asked me if I had spoken with my brothers recently and I mentioned that Jack had unexpectedly yelled at me.

"Oh, about your mother?" Oskar intuitively asked.

"Yes," I said.

I was relieved as Oskar calmly continued, "Everyone has their own experiences," validating both Jack and me at the same time.

Jack said Oskar was smart.

So here is my previous partner in crime, Jack, flat out telling me I am delusional and my memories are nothing. Young Jack had survived my mother too, but adult Jack is still influenced by her. As kids, I remember us casually commenting between ourselves that he 'got it the worst' from my mother. But here he was emphatically stating that "Mom was a good mom and she loved us."

I don't know about Jack's mental health now, but when we were children he used to cry and wish he were dead because of the way my mother treated him. I don't remember what she did to him, I only remember his reactions. Maybe he forgot? I'd certainly believe it if he said he did forget. Little kids don't have suicidal ideations without cause.

My conversation with Jack illuminates how easy it is to discredit people who have been oppressed and traumatized—I had done it to myself too. It also further exemplifies the consequences of trauma in his irrational anger and meanness towards me whether my mother had had a hand in his rant or not. This young man has been made to believe that he is a bad person when he is not, and this has been done to him through oppressive manipulation. If people have been traumatized or oppressed, they don't feel safe and can act crazy and even turn violent. In our common circumstance, I have more often directed this violence against myself; whereas, in this scenario, Jack was directing his anger at me. *Jack, I wish neither of us would be violent or angry towards ourselves or each other. So maybe I have 'gone soft' as you suggested. But you will always be the beautiful boy I know in my heart, no matter how angry you get.*

We cannot know another person's experience, but if someone exhibits a lack of empathy or acts inhumanely towards themselves or others, it would be to our benefit to be cognizant that there is a reason for it. The police might still need to be called, but a mindset of compassionate empathy is a tremendously powerful tool for dealing with hurt people. When I witness people acting out of character or without empathy, I first consider what happened to them to make them act a certain way. The wonder-drug of basic human relativity can help stave off socially risky states of mental illness, as human relativity has done for me, and also for Jack and Owen.

Jack cannot hear me and sadly that means we cannot get to know each other again quite yet. I hope some time in the future Jack will want to get to know me, instead of essentially telling me, "Vada, you don't know jack."

Jack, I patiently wait to fill in the blanks of the good times we had growing up. I know they exist; I can feel them, and I think they are abundant. You are about the only person who can jog my memory on this one. In the meantime, I wait... and maybe those memories will resurface more clearly on their own, as so many have, and I can be the happy reminiscer.

CHAPTER 47

S Ave E

The internet has made the world small. I was hoping Babo was dead or back in Korea, but I readily searched to find out that he operates a bookshop at the same location where Beescrit Books had left him, South Avenue East, under a different bookshop name. For the sake of humanity, I was sincerely hoping Babo was gone from this Earth.

Don't worry, Babo; I won't hurt a damn fly if I can help it. I hate you, Babo, and I don't like hating you. I hate you, Babo, for making me hate you. Get your flame retardant gear ready, buddy, you're going to hell if there is one. I know your behavior is the consequence of fucked up shit you did not ask for, but it does not excuse you for abusing me or anyone else. I know you are not responsible for becoming a monster, Babo, but you did become one. I know you don't care. I asked for an apology from you once and you said you didn't know what I was talking about.

Babo acquired the bookshop from Beescrit Books.

Beescrit admittedly knows Babo is a predator because human resources confirmed it with me directly: "That is why we removed Babo from Beescrit Books."

HR failed to mention that they had made a business arrangement out of Babo's departure. Beescrit and Itchee knowingly allowed a predatory abuser to walk free. The bookshop changed hands, and Beescrit knew full-well what type of person would be interacting with the public at South Avenue East. *Beescrit gee-doe-jahs, take a hard look and read between the lines. Beescrit does not care about you; they care far more about money. Anything for a buck.*

CHAPTER 48

Cirque de Beescrit

Mountain top where Itchee was "enlightened"

I didn't know Itchee-Ree very well, the ringleader of the Beescrit Books' circus. Itchee kept his distance. *Smart move, buddy.* I have always said that smart plus any negative quality is dangerous. I cannot say much about Itchee, except he heads an organization that enslaves people. The Beescrit Books circus is akin to human trafficking and slavery.

Itchee-Ree arrived in the United States in 1988 at Laguardia International Airport, after having been *enlightened* in 1984. As Itchee tells the story, he comes with the clothes on his back, one special tunic for leading spiritual training, $5K cash, and a dream of a better world. At the airport, Itchee finds himself curious and excited to be in the United States, so excited that he walks away from his luggage. A man appears in Itchee's face speaking in "speedy English" and waving his hands. Itchee doesn't speak English, or so he claims... *Still not quite sure how Itchee could not learn English, considering how frequently he hears his own words translated into English in real time in his hours-long lectures. I picked up Korean over the years by listening. I was scolded for understanding Korean and had to pretend I did not. ...*So this guy is in Itchee's face talking fast. Itchee gets a feeling something was off, turns back toward his luggage, and sees another man running off with it. Itchee turns back towards the first man—of the waving arms—but he is gone too.

"I could have really been down on my luck," Itchee quips inspirationally with good humor.

Itchee next phones his student, residing in the US, who would be taking him in to stay at his home. Itchee pondered his situation at his student's house. He could have easily given up on his dreams. Instead, Itchee decided to take the high road. *Such a noble human being!*

"I gave a donation to New York City," Itchee proudly states amidst conveying the story. "I was so generous I didn't even keep a penny for myself. What if I had given up?" Itchee asks his students. *The guy thinks he's funny.*

Itchee's students are grateful he overcame such obstacles to give them the opportunity to grow their souls through Beescrit Books for Wellness. *Yeah, yeah, yeah! Whatever.*

Itchee has been in jail in Korea. He is forthcoming with the information, and explains how he was incorrectly charged and imprisoned for multiple criminal acts. *Beescrit gee-doe-jahs: Charles Manson's followers also wrote him letters when he was in jail and even camped outside the courthouse during his trial.*

Itchee tells the story of how Beescrit Books came to be: He grew up in an impoverished village in Korea... I actually visited the village myself once... Itchee had a learning disability and found little meaning in his life. One day, Itchee decided to make use of himself and move all the stinky garbage from under the bridge in his small town out to the hills. Itchee used the trash as fertilizer and planted watermelon seeds. Everyone in the village was happy about the watermelons and the cleaned-up trash.

Despite his challenges, Itchee had magical experiences in childhood, including dashing off into a winter storm to get food for his family. Itchee made it through the snowstorm in record time, unscathed, as if he had flown to the market and back.

He then took up martial arts with a passion. He fastened weights on his limbs to make it harder to fight and to expend his energy. *Sounds to me like Itchee may have had some anger issues? Ahem, TRAUMA.* Anywho, Itchee became obsessed with martial arts and meditation. He claims that he sat in the snow one day in meditation for a long while. When he came out of it he was frozen and could not move. Accepting his imminent death, he sensed all at once a heat move through his body, melting the snow around him. He also spent a month on a mountain top without eating or sleeping so as to attain *enlightenment.* I visited this mountain top where he was supposedly enlightened. Coming down from the mountain, Itchee was ready to do what he needed in order to share his enlightenment: he left his wife and children. *Hmmm, okay...*

Itchee's Beescrit beginnings are unimpressive, starting with his performing simple body movements in a public park in Korea. A small group of people joined in on these free park exercises regularly. Next, he rented a place for practicing movement and meditation indoors and started writing spiritual books. At first, Itchee divided ownership of the rented space among his enlightenment practice partners. He says his shared ownership did not work out because people fought over who should do the menial tasks, each person believing he was above another. Itchee asked his "partners" to sign a paper stating they would not use the meditation methods and enlightenment techniques imparted in his books for their own financial benefit or business. Most people would not sign and left. A few of the most devoted remained with Itchee. The business became a public bookshop offering daily self-help classes. The bookshop expanded to several locations, and then Itchee decided he would share his enlightenment with the whole United States. *Did Itchee even really have money in the bag stolen at Laguardia?*

Gee-doe-jahs in Beescrit cannot be told that they are part of a cult and have been fooled. It is more than terrifying to accept the reality, so the brain protects cult members through denial. The power of manipulative money-hungry people is an added inhibitor for cult members to accurately perceive reality. Beescrit provides experiential proof, science, art, photographs, and completely fabricated charts to support their philosophies. It is remarkable gaslighting. Cult members believe the Beescrit notion that "negative talk" within the institution itself is worthless and damaging. *But it's not true. We have those emotions and thoughts for a reason. Repeatedly rejecting our internal messages that signal danger leaves us incapable of discerning what is safe and what is not; likewise, repeatedly rejecting inclinations of our likes and dislikes denies our discernment of what is true for us and what is false.* People have dedicated their lives to Beescrit and Itchee-Ree. They are being abused; they don't know it, and to them their abusers seem virtuous. Their lights have been tamped out and their nervous systems are malfunctioning. *Battering oneself can do that! Authorities, please help them. The CIA has a file on Itchee-Ree for certain.*

Beescrit Books has grown into an international company with various affiliates operating as for-profit as well as non-profit organizations. The places where Beescrit and these affiliates operate and run classes include: retail space in small towns and big cities—their parks, and their kids' schools; corporate lunch rooms, and assisted living complexes and nursing homes. Beescrit is associated with the United Nations, holds ties with various governments, and more. Itchee-Ree even held a conference at the United Nations once. I attended, held a door for an eminent brain scientist who shall remain nameless.

Of course, brainwashing presents miracles! The brain is indeed a wondrous place and has tremendous power to survive. When a person is repetitively bombarded, the brain will eventually collapse and succumb to whatever it needs in order to function in a given environment. I've claimed that Beescrit Books is a microcosm of various convoluted systems of oppression; the macrocosm is collective society. The people in the worst scenario in Beescrit shape-shift like contortionists between being a wolf and being a sheep, as necessary, depending on their environment, responsibilities, and requisite etiquette.

Itchee, scratch that shit. I'm pointing you out. I'll do the middle finger, instead of index for you, buddy.

BEESCRIT 'TRUE TEACHER' / ITCHEE REE

CHAPTER 49

Fall From Grace

ANOTHER WORLD

As I conclude writing this memoir, the connective bits of my past have been revealing themselves to me for sixteen months. I would have forgotten a lot of the information contained in this book if I hadn't written it down. The part of me that has habitually denied the abuse I have suffered still whitewashes it out of my mind much of the time. It is particularly difficult to accept that my mother abused me. My body, however, embodies all that has happened. Part of me yearns to kindle more memories of my mother so that I can better understand the inexplicable terror that my body has suffered. *But I guess I am still not ready for that.* Beside the radiant warmth of smoldering internal embers of a traumatic past, I am also reminded of good times with safe people. I will stop everything to bask in a warm recollection that comes to mind of my grandparents, a moment of camaraderie with Jack, or the strumming sound of Clyde's guitar that sometimes syncs with my surroundings because, despite the grief and tragic loss, remembering makes me feel more whole and connected. I also find it easier to put my anger where it belongs.

My mother remains largely absent in my accumulated recollections. I have a lot of mixed feelings about her. I'd be angry if I learned that anyone had been treated the way Grace has treated me. I am not an angry person, but I am angry about what happened to me. I grieve lost love and the fact that the trauma symptoms I cope with could have been avoided if my mother hadn't been a psychopath. However, I also feel liberated by knowing the truth. I don't have to hate myself anymore because of the lies Grace made me believe about myself. It is a load off my soul. With my anger appropriately placed, I still don't hate Grace because in a lot of ways she still doesn't exist to me. Like anyone else in this world, I do not wish her ill. And she's probably still got on her sundress and southern hospitality for her public… When I imagine a mother having a true sense of competition against her own child though… That's some dark shit. I wouldn't wish Grace's mental illness on anyone. It seems too terrible.

Will Grace continue to convince her peeps how horrible and crazy I am? I am giving her a lot of good content to use against me by publishing this book. It is probably either one of the stupidest things I will ever do, or one of the smartest.

When I was young in my alone time, I built a world for myself that has beautiful trees, magic, and happiness—my first world. It's actually more of a feeling than anything else. Grace built another world for me that has monsters, devils, and mass confusion—my second world. Reality can be pretty magical too I think, even with its shadows.

Grace is not only a villain; she is also a victim of the dire effects of social oppression and generational trauma. I still have to cry wolf for little Vada though. Grace broke my brain and left me to the rest of the wolf pack. Mothers don't do that. Thanks to my resilience I survived. Thanks to my resilience no one noticed what was happening with me. I fought my battles in perfect people-pleasing pitch and as authentically as it gets. Grace hoped I'd forgotten the earliest diablerie, and I had, but I remember enough of the ugly truth to know that for me she is a dangerous person. She has lied to me my whole life, all the while professing her love for me. Nurturing a relationship with her seems unlikely. I have to fall from Grace.

During Jack's angry phone rant, he stated that I am just like Grace. I have always been terrified of that. I remind myself of her in the ways I look and talk, the jokes I make—and I realize now that I have feared myself because of it. But I finally know that in essence I am nothing like her. Through self-awareness one can adjust and correct. Genetics aside, a daughter can choose mindfully not to repeat her mother's bad behaviors.

Grace, I am sorry for whatever life events caused you to abandon yourself. My role in your theater has expired. Give me the curtain hook and yank me off your stage.

CHAPTER 50

Ground To Stand On

OSKAR

i think i was
a good baby,
you could not
have guessed
anything
was wrong

My father has called me almost every day since my car accident back in 2016, but it is still very hard for Oskar and me to talk about my childhood trauma, so we mostly do not. Oskar is always here for me though, supporting me in any way he can. And, to me, that's what counts.

Oskar, I am still not sure you know what your support means to me. Everything. Your support gives me ground to stand on. Your acceptance of my symptoms and my reality, and your support in getting me help now are giving me a chance at a healthy relationship with myself and interpersonally and in society.

Nightmares every night, dissociation throughout the day with flashbacks, emotional flashbacks from across time and space occurring mid-conversation, hitting myself in the most stressful interpersonal situation, and then suicidal ideations—how long can a person go on like that? There seems no time for anything else other than trying to recover from all those symptoms and it's no life. Oskar believed me when I told him I needed extra care, even when he did not completely understand my situation. And because of that, I had a fighting chance. It has been a lot of work on my part, but I finally came out on top of the heap.

Oskar amped up his dad-game when my memories started coming back. I visited him for Father's Day. Oskar skipped church to spend time with me.

"We will go get sandwiches," Oskar said, "spending time together is what we need to do."

I noticed that both he and my step-mother, Miranda, made special efforts to find me at the Father's Day afternoon barbecue to spend time with me and have conversations. Oskar and Miranda asked about statements I made and ideas I presented, then listened, giving me a healthy dose of *human relativity* as I had just commenced fleshing out the concept of my book. On the drive home, I felt the comfort of their human relativity settle within me and was frankly surprised how effective it was. Their human relativity substantially lingered inside of me, changing me for the better long after I had left the barbecue. I felt that I'd been seen and heard, and because of this, unusually safe.

Oskar, I love you. I feel lucky you are my father. Not sure we would have crossed paths otherwise, and what a shame that would have been.

CHAPTER 51

Don't Forget

I thought there was an ultimate truth to which I was not yet privy. Now I realize there are likely as many truths as there are people in the world.

My brothers are very important to me. My brother Owen has loved me generously; he is intelligent and my type of funny. I am proud of him. He has overcome his hurdles like a stallion on steroids. My brother Jack remains the love of my life. I initially thought that I had abandoned him, and I am sad that I have missed out on time with Jack that I can never get back. After remembering Jack more precisely in a wider timeframe, I understand Jack was not my responsibility. Geographically, Jack got space from Grace but not before she really screwed with his head. *Jack, Mom is a liar. The times she treated us like shit are private. If anyone were to have witnessed this, they would plainly see we were under attack, especially when we were children. We would have been taken away from her if anyone knew how she treated us. Mom lied, Jack; we are not the bad ones. She is the bad one.*

I thought maybe I'd never know myself and I'd be forever divided inside, compartmentalizing and forgetting with an indistinguishably pleasant face to the world. And on the inside I was more like a deer in headlights, prematurely surrendering her attention to the stars above. Developmental Trauma informed psychotherapy combined with Neurofeedback therapy have matched a wizardry to charm a result in me that is magical. Brand my forehead with a thunderbolt, remove the cloak of invisibility, and call me Harry Potter—I can finally see myself! I now understand why people like me; it is because I am a beautiful person.

There have been many departures in my life, so I am pretty good at goodbyes and we are coming up to one.

I witnessed an interaction between a young boy and his mother at a local pharmacy. I was in the waiting area. They were headed into the restroom. The mother held the bathroom door for the boy. The boy hesitated, and the mother noticed his quick, nearly imperceptible moment of hesitation.

She quickly glanced at their surroundings, looked at the boy, and said, "Be a big boy and wait for me here, okay?"

I could tell the boy was happy and bolstered by a subtle confidence as he headed into the men's restroom by himself and then patiently waited afterwards for his mother just outside its doors. *What a beautiful interaction.* Mostly without words, the mother and the boy had communicated. I watched the subtle clues between them and the way the mother helped the boy safely stretch into individuality by allowing him to use the restroom by himself when he felt ready.

Vada could be anyone you meet. Vada could be the person sitting in the waiting area at your local pharmacy. Vada could be any gender, any color, any age. Vada could be a stranger or a friend. I lived a whole life and no one saw me. Probably because I could not see myself.

Who is Vada Broz? I apparently held tight to goodness against all odds. I am grateful for the continuous reduction of symptoms under the right care for my mental health; less dissociation, nightmares almost entirely gone, flashbacks are more like memories instead of virtual reality thrill rides, suicidal ideations are drastically reduced, and I haven't hit myself at all since I started Neurofeedback. Though I faced my mother's cruelty from the moment I was born, Grace succeeded at giving me a better life and environment than she herself has had. I still can't figure out how I became smart—maybe it was all the Sesame Street or afternoons spent in the library reading encyclopedias and books on nature when I was a kid. The people who met me with human relativity embossed my kindness; therefore, miraculously, my capacity to love remains intact, and here I am.

I never knew the value of human relationships and their place within the integrity of society. I thought everything interpersonal was destined to fail, and I didn't even know I thought that way. But it's not true. I have found beauty in relationships. Real growth happens in real life, not in a linear fashion but in an interactive one. We are evolving as a planet of people. It is happening whether we like it or not, and the direction of our evolution is in our hands. I am asking to make meaning of my suffering by reducing our mutual suffering. We need to pull the wool from our eyes, and be a kind stranger with some human relativity when we can. Acts of kindness or decent human relativity can potentially save individuals and ourselves from acts of violence and hate, small and large.

Speaking of kind strangers, a mysterious and wise stranger wrote me this note in a coffee shop circa 2013 following my *exit* from Beescrit: Vada, don't forget to draw and also calm the fuck down. It was signed, Tyler.

I almost did forget to draw! And I had actually 'forgotten' so many things. *Thank you, Tyler, whoever and wherever you are.* If not for kind strangers and good people, this would be a very different story.

ACKNOWLEDGMENTS

And Thanks

Dusty in an amnesic library and dated twenty years back were her novel insights into *The Great Gatsby...*

Flying off the shelves in the abandoned archives of my mind, there had been disorienting apparitions of terror and foggy visions of interactions so tender they nearly broke my heart. *What were the reflections of this English teacher doing here?*

I couldn't place her name or see her face, but I recalled her voice, her blonde hair, and her intense passion for literature. I discerned a distinct intelligence due to her unique ability to read between the lines—a quality that I knew my memoir could benefit from. More memories crept in revealing her kindness, warmth, and cheerful humor; as well as, how she wore bulky sweaters and kept her chalk in her pockets.

Forty thousand words and a pile of pictures. I knew early in my writing process that I would need an editor who could shoulder the heaviness of my story. This person would have to be someone I could trust, and of course I wanted her to be brilliant. And so it was at forty thousand words into transcribing my amnesic archives, that the insightful chalk-pocketing lover of literature had made her presence known through a series of flashbacks. *Now what in the heck was her name?*

Months passed, my writing had accumulated to ninety-five thousand words, and my mission was clear. *Now I really needed an editor and, if my memory had served me right, I was by this time convinced that this woman was the perfect candidate.* After some investigation, I found her name, her face, and eventually her home phone number.

Mrs. Quote had resigned from my alma mater, but when we connected on the phone she spoke of what she had been doing most recently in her spare time—comparing Shakespeare's

Hamlet and *The Tempest. Not exactly light reading. Of course, I thought this was wonderful because my story weighed a ton.* Her words also confirmed her genuine fascination with literature as I had inferred about her from my flashbacks. She didn't remember me without a face to go with it, but she was happy to take a look at the work of a former student. *Yip!*

I sent Mrs. Quote the original version of this memoir in its rawest form. It was an absolute mess of time and space because amnesia doesn't clear linearly. She offered thoughtful constructive criticism about the manuscript without having read it word for word. She kindly and discreetly pointed out what was developmentally amiss as well as some certain strengths that had potential. She suggested I find someone with familiarity in the field of psychology for editing and politely declined to undertake it herself. *This response frankly only reinforced my convictions about her.*

Using her critique as a guide, I tore the original version apart and restructured its content. *She had given me precisely what I needed.* In this stroke of *heroic destiny* (as she would call it), I asked her if she would take a look at the new version. It was one of the most thrilling moments of my life when she replied with her terms for editing it.

She polished every detail of my efforts. Her dedication to preserving my words and meaning was mystifying—I sometimes thought she had a magic wand. When it served the integrity of the work as literature or mission, Mrs. Quote generously proffered her own inspiration to enhance them. She was respectful in regard to my vulnerability and maneuvered my cumbersome story with sophistication. I sincerely thank her for making this a better book in the end than it was at its start.

I would also like to acknowledge my therapist Noah for his steady support, especially in my most haunting moments. I thank my father Oskar for believing in me and standing by me. I am grateful to the innumerable friends who have supported me in various ways throughout my life, including those not mentioned in this book. Thanks to Evelyn, since it was our tumultuous relationship that forced me to face my shadows. Thanks to my beach buddy and guiding light John for being just a phone call away, always ready to listen, laugh, or cry with me. Thanks to Jane for validating my story even when it invalidated her own experience. And finally thanks to Maeve for our rare and invaluable friendship—*I'm so glad we met.*

LIST OF ILLUSTRATIONS

CPSIA information can be obtained
at www.ICGtesting.com
Printed in the USA
LVHW080241071122
732524LV00013B/1148